THE *Business* ADVISOR

T0362963

GLOBAL
PUBLISHING
G R O U P

Global Publishing Group

Australia • New Zealand • Singapore • America • London

THE
Business
ADVISOR

THE INSIDER GUIDE TO TRANSFORM YOUR BUSINESS TO HAVE MORE CASH, CUSTOMERS AND CLIENTS

THU LE HUYNH

First Edition 2020

National Library of Australia
Cataloguing-in-Publication entry:

The Business Advisor. The Insider Guide to Transform your Business to Have More Cash, Customers and Clients - Thu Le Huynh

1st ed.
ISBN: 978-1-925288-90-2 (pbk.)

A catalogue record for this book is available from the National Library of Australia

Published by Global Publishing Group
PO Box 517 Mt Evelyn, Victoria 3796 Australia
Email Info@GlobalPublishingGroup.com.au

For further information about orders:
Phone: +61 3 9726 4133

*I dedicate this book to those of you
making your dreams and goals come true.*

*"The world values the seer above all men,
and has always done so. Nay, it values all
men in proportion as they partake of the
character of seers. The Elgin Marbles and
a decision of John Marshall are valued
for the same reason. What we feel in
them is a painstaking submission to facts
beyond the author's control, and to ideas
imposed upon him by his vision."*

John Jay Chapman

ACKNOWLEDGEMENTS

Firstly, I would like to acknowledge a number of very important people in various part of my life in the order that we crossed paths. My late parents who encouraged me to get an education. My father had always instilled in me the importance of schooling. Looking back now I can see how much value he placed on education and I'm glad, because it's served me well. They gave me the freedom to make my own decisions as a child because they wanted to make sure I'd be okay if anything ever happened and they were no longer around.

My brothers, sisters, brothers in-law, sisters in-law, Simon, Sunrise and Sasha have continued to play important roles throughout my life. I am grateful for the happiness memories and support.

Sabine Isbarn and dog Paddy. One day at the Altone Park I saw this gorgeous white dog with big blue eyes (he looked just like a toy) scamper away whimpering as soon as he spotted my dog Simon, because of Simon's size. Sabine and I got talking and became great friends. She told me she had completed a taxation course. Several years later I went back to Curtin University to start a Master of Taxation and changed career.

Maureen Luca is a great long-term friend who gives wise advice and helps review various important documents including this book, and helps me in business.

Sherly Sanjaya is a wonderful friend who encouraged me to have a business. I appreciate you for your help.

Liana Ciufo, Pippa and Chuckey are marvellous in looking after Sasha when I am away for training and when I was writing this book. Thank you for taking the time to help me.

Thank you so much to my Publisher Global Publishing Group and their team for their guidance and support that makes the process an easier and enjoyable one.

CONTENTS

CHAPTER 1

BUILD A SOLID FOUNDATION FOR YOUR BUSINESS

CHAPTER 1

BUILD A SOLID FOUNDATION FOR YOUR BUSINESS

> *"You are today where your thoughts have brought you.*
> *You will be tomorrow where your thoughts take you."*
> **James Lane Allen**

The concept of building your business is similar to building your house. Building a house is easy, but humans are more complex. The house needs a strong foundation to withstand stormy weather and prevent a sinkhole. Your business needs to have a strong foundation to weather various cycles and the influences of the economy.

In reality, business can change your life for better or worse. Some businesses are successful, some businesses will struggle to survive, and some businesses go bankrupt.

Here are some of the common reasons people get into business:

1. Need to have a business to get the work

2. To be their own boss and in control of their business outcomes

3. Tax benefits

4. Flexible working hours

5. Security

6. Pride

7. Tired of getting nowhere with their career.

8. More time

9. Innovation

10. No politics

11. Their area of expertise and passion

12. Become wealthy in a short period of time

13. Make a name for themselves

When is the best time to start your business?

This is a tough question. It depends on the business owner's situation at the time.

For example, I started my business in 2009, and I found out at one of the business seminars I attended that I started my business during a recession. The presenter said that the best time to start a business is during a recession because if your business can survive it, then it will survive good times too.

Getting into business is not right for everyone because there is a lot involved, including cash reserves, qualification, insurance, products and services, plant and equipment, training, marketing and sales, staff, business structure, the business name, logo, business premises, terms and conditions, software systems and policy, various laws, etc.

1. **Finance**

    In business money can go out a lot quicker than it is coming in. Some businesses need a lot of money to start with, and have a lot more operating expenses than other businesses. Some business owners start a business and also have a part-time job to support its cashflow. Some business owners have to take out their superannuation to pay for their business expenses and the purchase of plant and equipment. Some business owners sell their two-storey house to support a business that makes no profit, or even a loss. However, there are also some very successful businesses making a great profit as well.

2. **Business name and logo**

    It is best to have a business name that reflects what your business does and what you stand for. Your logo should be simple but send the right message and image to the public. A business name can be a marketing tool. Your business name and image can speak thousands of words.

3. **Laws**

    It is expected that the business owner and the taxpayer know about their responsibilities and obligations. For example, in a company structure it is required by ASIC that directors meet the responsibilities of management of the affairs of the company. The director also needs to obey the required tax and superannuation laws to prevent or minimise personal liability.

4. **Business structure**

    Most business owners have the luxury of deciding the best business structure for their business. However, there are some business owners who have no choice in selecting the most suitable structure for them because another party's terms and conditions may require them to set up a particular company structure in order to do business with them.

    The four most common business structures in Australia are sole trader, company, trust and partnership. A sole trader business is the simplest, with minimal costs to setup; however it does not offer asset protection. If you want asset protection, then either select a company, or a corporate trustee with a trust structure. The cost of setting up a trust or company is a lot more than for setting up a sole trader. If you are not sure which business structure is best for you and your business, it is best to seek advice from a qualified tax professional or lawyer. This advice may cost you several hundred dollars, but it can save you from making costly mistakes and help avoid headaches in the future.

Here are some of the factors to consider which make selecting the right business structure important:

1. Cost of setting it up
2. Complexity of structure
3. Asset protection and liability
4. Wealth creation
5. Capital gains tax consequences
6. Tax obligations
7. Accountant's fee for preparing and lodging tax returns
8. Commercial laws
9. Tax laws
10. Corporation laws
11. Payroll laws

5. Business premises and location

Whether you have a physical business premises depends on the type of business. For example restaurants need a business premises, great food and service and a great location does help to attract more customers into the restaurants.

We are living in the time where fast internet and technology enable people to carry out their business worldwide. They can do their work on the beach, during travelling, in an airport, at a café, etc. This means we can provide mobile service or service over the laptop without leaving our home or office. All you need is a good laptop and good internet connection. This is very cost effective as you don't need to pay high rent, don't need to hire staff to stay in the office, and you have flexible working hours.

6. Business action plan

"Three men were laying brick.
The first was asked: "What are you doing?"
He answered: "Laying some brick."
The second man was asked: "What are you working for?"
He answered: "Five dollars a day."
The third man was asked: "What are you doing?"
He answered: "I am helping to build a great cathedral."
Which man are you?
Charles M. Schwab

A good business plan should be part of business management and it should be reviewed and updated regularly. Before you write a business plan, you need to determine the reason you want one and the outcome you want to achieve, so you know which type of business plan you need to write. There are a number of different kinds, depending on what you plan to use and accomplish. Different situations call for different types of business plans. An effective one will match its intended use.

Here are a few common business plans:

- A simple plan is a one-page business plan of your goals, rewards, deadlines, milestones and budget. It is quick, easy and more effective than a formal business plan. This plan is most useful when you want to grow your business.

- A start-up business plan includes projected start-up costs, start-up steps, plant and equipment, vehicles, amount of capital needed, marketing, profit and loss, balance sheet, cashflow, feasibility plan, contingency plan, staff, strengths and weaknesses.

- A standard business plan is required when you need to present a plan to a bank to obtain funding.

- A marketing plan – in which you determine your revenue goal then work out the number of leads you want, the conversion rate and the sales. The best way is to work backwards.

It is important to have a business plan; it is like a GPS for your business. However, your business plan should be practical and not too many pages. It needs to be continually updated, it is not a document that you file away and forget about.

7. **Terms and conditions**

There is great benefit in using the services of a commercial lawyer to create the terms and conditions document for your business, because it can protect your assets, reduce your chances of getting bad debts, meet the legal requirements, and ensure the best outcome in the event of a court situation.

8. **Systems and processes**

Setting out systems and processes is an ongoing work of progress. As your business changes, find better ways of doing things.

9. **Software**

A business may use a number of different types of software. Where possible, invest in the most suitable technology and software for your business; this will save hours of time, money, and may prevent you from getting a penalty.

Let's look at the two most common ways business owner do their bookkeeping: shoebox receipts and the cloud bookkeeping software.

The shoebox receipts method is very common for start-up businesses. However, it can be very time consuming for the owner to sort out the receipts to prepare the Business Activity Statement and tax return. It is costly to pay for bookkeeping to sort out the receipts, to manually enter the transactions in the software, do the reconciliation, etc. In some cases, the Australian Taxation Office (ATO) may penalise the business owner several hundred dollars for each late return lodgement.

Cloud bookkeeping software can be set up to automate major bookkeeping tasks. Some software has a business insight chart to help track and monitor income and expenses. Depending on the software and the subscription level, some software can be used on laptops and mobile phones to upload invoices, receipts, as well as allowing invoicing on the go, and enabling customers to pay by credit card, bPay and by online transfer.

Some business owners may make incorrect assumptions about software without actually analysing the final outcome. For example, cloud bookkeeping may appear an expensive investment, but the actual outcome may be a lot less expensive than you think when compared to other methods. As you know, technology does play up now and then, needing maintenance and updates, therefore it is important to select a software provider which has a reliable and friendly technical support team that you can call for help if needed.

10. Plant and equipment

The plant and equipment depends on the products and services provided.

11. Products and services

Some business owners may conduct market research to see how many people are interested in buying their products and services.

12. Insurance

Insurers can reduce your risk provided you tell them exactly the situation of your business, and do not install any plant or equipment that they specify they won't cover.

An example of this from our research and the ABC News is the case where "Wangara Factory Fire Damage Bill Tipped To Hit $12M." The manufacturer was destroyed by fire at about 10.20am on August 22, 2015, and it was not insured.

13. Protect your business and your money from scammers

Learn to recognise scammer's emails, text, letters and phone calls so that you don't waste your precious time and lose money to scammers. Some scammers pretend to be ASIC (Australian Securities and Investments Commission) or ATO (Australia Taxation Office) asking you to pay a fee of a different amount than your invoice, and to provide your bank details and personal information in order to renew your business or receive a refund.

Listed below are a few ways you can tell if an email or phone call is likely to be a scam:

- the sender's email address looks strange
- when you click the link in the email and it goes to a strange link or different email address
- when you are asked to make a payment over the phone or by email
- when you are asked to make a payment in order to receive a refund
- if they ask for your credit card or bank details by email or over the phone
- when you are asked to pay fees that are a different amount to the invoice amount

In these situations, you can contact the relevant organisation or supplier to check whether it is a scam email. You can report the scammer to ASIC, ATO or ACCC (Australian Competition and Consumer Commission). They then warn the community of the latest scams, which helps other people. The ACCC is unable to recover any money lost to a scammer, or help track down a scammer. Here is a list of recent scam alerts taken from ato.gov. au/scams:

Latest alerts:

- June 2019 – fake tax debt scam via WhatsApp
- May 2019 SMS scam – tax refund notification
- April 2019 phone scam – imitating ATO phone numbers
- March 2019 email scam – myGov tax refund notification
- September 2018 phone scam – fake tax agent
- July 2018 email scam – ATO impersonation
- May 2018 text message scam – fake tax refund
- March 2018 phone scam – voicemail
- March 2018 email scam – tax refund review
- February 2018 email scam – tax refund notification
- January 2018 phone scam – fake tax refund
- January 2018 email scam – tax form
- December 2017 phone scam – fake debts
- September 2017 email scam – refund
- August 2017 scam – tax return form
- July 2017 email scam – tax repayment
- March 2017 email Scam – online activity statement

In summary

Every business will experience problems from time to time. These may be in a number of areas including internet, software, plant and equipment, customers, suppliers and staff. It is important to have a technical support team, and various other business support teams, that you can call on for help as needed. It is too much to expect a business owner to know every aspect of running a business. This is an impossible goal to achieve and it's not the best use of the business owner's time. Many business owners make the mistake of taking on too many non-productive tasks at the expenses of their other higher priority business goals. More importantly, they are not getting the outcomes they want. They spend hours learning "How to…". The business owner should spend more time adding a team of experts to their business so they have the right person to get the job done.

It is vital that your business foundation is built correctly, in order to have a successful business. If not, you may have to rebuild or start over which can be a very expensive and exhausting process.

Here are the key points:
1. Cash is the king of business to help you pay your staff, yourself and suppliers.
2. Marketing is the queen of business to help you continue getting sales
3. Get a business structure
4. Analyse products and services
5. Analyse and update systems and policies
6. Get the right team
7. Protect your business and money from scammers

CHAPTER 2

THE 3D'S OF BUSINESS OWNERS – DISEASE, DIVORCE AND DEATH

"There are three marks of a superior man:

being virtuous, he is free from anxiety;

being wise, he is free from perplexity;

being brave, he is free from fear."

Confucius

CHAPTER 2

THE 3D'S OF BUSINESS OWNERS – DISEASE, DIVORCE AND DEATH

> *"We have long had death and taxes as the two standards of inevitability. But there are those who believe that death is the preferable of the two."*
> **Erwin N. Griswold**

Not every business owner has to face the 3D's. Everyone has to face death one day, unfortunately no one knows the exact date in the future. It is better to plan in advance while you still have a sound mind, early in life, to avoid any unforeseen unfortunate situations which may arise suddenly. It is not easy to talk about this topic but you should have legal documents prepared in advance. It will be more difficult for your family if something happens to you and there has been no planning – including estate planning, your will, medical power of attorney, medical and lifestyle power of attorney, and enduring power of attorney – put in place. If there is no pre-planning, no safeguards in place, or if you leave it too late, unforeseen situations may mean that you are no longer able to make decisions yourself. This means you don't have a say in how you want to live the remainder of your life – the government and courts may make the decisions for you. Your family also have to deal with the stress, and the emotional and financial changes to their lifestyle. It is also a good idea to review these documents on a regular basis to ensure that you are still happy with the decisions you made and it is up-to date with current laws.

Estate planning

The following information is taken from the ATO website "Estate planning involves developing a strategy to deal with your assets after you die – the legal instruments and structures, such as a will, you put in place to transfer your assets in the event of death. Tax is a major consideration in estate planning, and strong governance relating to the tax aspects of estate administration can help manage the risks. Ensure you or your staff have sufficient knowledge and skills to meet your responsibilities. Be prepared to seek assistance from external advisers on more complex tax issues."

Proper estate planning includes planning for financial, medical and lifestyle changes. For example, estate planning ensures assets are kept in the blood-line; the beneficiary may worry the marriage won't last, or when they pass the money will not go to their children, or the right person is not getting the money. You may have a testamentary trust as a way of asset protection, and tax planning to minimise the risk for the beneficiaries. It is best to seek legal advice to ensure that the trust is properly established for serving its purpose, and in order to determine whether the trust income is enough to pay for the ongoing administrative fees required to maintain the trust.

Findlaw.com's "What is a testamentary trust and should I have one?" states that a testamentary trust is established under a will and comes into effect after the death of the person making the will.

The benefits of having this trust including:

1. The trustee has the discretion to distribute capital and income to the beneficiaries

2. They have asset protection because the assets belong to the trust, not the beneficiaries. A testamentary trust can be used to protect assets in the following situations:

- In shaky relationships or even divorce relationship situations, where there is a worry that the marriage may not last. In these events, in the case of a beneficiary, the assets belong to the trust, so the Family Court will not consider these assets as belonging to an individual. It is therefore not part of the distribution, and thus protects the inheritance assets.
- Creditor protection – if a beneficiary has several creditors with a potential high risk of bankruptcy.
- High-risk beneficiaries – the testamentary trust is useful where the beneficiary has a high-risk career or business and there is thus the possibility they may go bankrupt or they may be sued. The money and assets are protected in testamentary trust.

- Will challenge – the will cannot be challenged when they die.

3. Protection of beneficiaries in the following situations
- The beneficiaries receive their social security entitlement.
- If the beneficiaries have addictions, including being a spendthrift, and gambling or drug addictions
- Remarriage of a spouse – the testamentary trust is used in cases where the spouse may remarry and distribute the assets to the new family members, or take out a bad investment due to the influence of a new spouse.

4. Tax planning
   Under the trust laws, the trustee has the discretion to distribute the trust income to any potential beneficiaries. The trust can be very tax effective.

When is the right time to do estate planning?

The best time to plan your estate is now, so that you are not caught off-guard and unprepared like most people faced with incapacity, serious illness or death. This will give you peace of mind.

Will

The will is an important legal document. It sets out your wishes and decisions on how you want things to be handled when you are gone. It can protect your spouse, children and assets. Findlaw. com's "Top Ten Reasons to Have a Will" are as follows:

1. Estate distribution

   Will allows you to decide how you want to distribute your assets to minimise and prevent any family conflict about your estate.

2. Minor children

   If you have younger children you can document in the will whom should look after your children instead of letting the court make the decision to choose among the family members or appointed guardian.

3. Probate process

   All estates go through process, but having a will helps to speed up this process.

4. Estate taxes

   A will may reduce your estate taxes.

5. Estate wind up

   Executors are the administrators of your estate and have the responsibility of making sure that all bills are paid, to do your tax returns, cancel your credit cards, and inform the bank and others. Executors can be a family or non-family person who is honest and trustworthy.

6. Disinherit individuals
    In the will you can exclude certain people from inheriting your estate. If there is no will, your estate may be distributed to the wrong person or someone you don't want to inherit, such as a bitter ex-spouse.

7. Gifts and donations
    Check the current laws about making gifts and donations.

8. Legal challenges
    A will helps to minimise or prevent challenges by family members. There is a case of a son who received over $1 million from a wrongful death lawsuit and upon his death his father (not part of the son's life for over 32 years) inherited the whole estate. Close relatives and siblings were left empty-handed.

9. Updated will
    It is recommended that you should continually review and updated your will as needed especially in the event of births, deaths and divorce.

10. Planning for unknown
    We don't know if and when unexpected death or disability will occur, so it is best to prepare the estate planning and will before it's too late.

Enduring Power of Attorney

Enduring power of attorney is a legal document which allows you to appoint a person to make decisions about your assets. Choice. com.au's "Enduring power of attorney risks" has two different type of enduring power of attorney that you can grant:

1. General power of attorney is to allow someone else to make decisions of your financial life for a certain period in situations where you take extended travel, a long stay in hospital, or until you become incapacitated. This document is invalid if you become incapacitated.

2. Enduring power of attorney is to allow someone else to make decisions for your financial life indefinitely in the event that you are mentally or physically incapable of making financial decisions yourself.

Be very careful whom you grant the power of attorney to and take reasonable steps to ensure there is no conflict of interest, and that they are not able to legally gain from taking over your affairs. They should have a kind heart and take your wishes into consideration. There are plenty of cases involving conflicts and family flights.

Medical power of attorney

Medical power of attorney means you give authorisation to allow someone to make your health care decisions in the event you are too ill and can't make decisions for yourself.

Medical and Lifestyle power of attorney

Medical and lifestyle power of attorney means you allow someone to make decisions for your personal lifestyle, where you live and medical treatment in the event that you lose mental capacity and can't make decisions yourself.

CHAPTER 3

TAX AND TAX PLANNING STRATEGIES

"Friends and neighbours complain that taxes are indeed very heavy, and if those laid on by the government were the only ones we had to pay, we might more easily discharge them; but we have many others, and much more grievous to some of us. We are taxed twice as much by our idleness, three times as much by our pride, and four times as much by our folly."

Benjamin Franklin

CHAPTER 3

TAX AND TAX PLANNING STRATEGIES

> *"The hardest thing in the world to understand is the income tax."*
> **Albert Einstein**

A valid tax invoice

There are two types of sales invoice: Taxable sales of less than $1,000.00 and Taxable sales of $1,000.00 or more. The ATO requirements for a valid tax invoice are outlined below.

A valid tax invoice for taxable sales of less than $1,000 must show seven pieces of information:
1. the document is intended to be a tax invoice
2. the seller's identity such as business name
3. the seller's Australian business number (ABN)
4. the date the invoice was issued
5. a brief description of the items sold, including the quantity (if applicable) and the price or description of the services provided

6. the GST amount (if any) payable – this can be shown separately or, if the GST amount is exactly one-eleventh of the total price, with a statement which says 'Total price includes GST'

7. the extent to which each sale on the invoice is a taxable sale (that is, the extent to which each sale includes GST).

The second type of valid tax invoice is for sales of $1,000 or more. It must show the buyer's identity or ABN. This invoice shows eight pieces of information. See the screenshot taken from the ATO website.

Why it is important to have a valid tax invoice?

Because only a valid invoice allows you to claim a tax deduction, it is a good practice to check the ABN on the invoice to ensure that the invoice has the correct ABN.

Here is a case where contractors purposely used other business's ABNs to avoid declaring income and paying tax. In this case, the contractors used Bunnings' ABN, according to Smh.com.au's article "Bunnings caught up in massive tradie tax fraud amid calls for ABN overhaul."

"…Bunnings Warehouse's Australian Business Number is being used in more than 40 per cent of all ABNs quoted in the Northern Territory, according to Michael Andrew, the chair of Treasury's Black Economy Taskforce. It is potentially costing taxpayers hundreds of millions of dollars in missed revenue. Using the wrong ABN effectively allows an independent contractor or supplier to dodge paying tax on a transaction. With cash transactions especially, it is almost impossible for the Australian Tax Office to ensure tax has been paid correctly…. when people ask for an invoice or a valid receipt they get the name of the company but they then get an ABN of someone else such as Bunnings… result of which is you can't trace where the money really went…Eleven-digit ABNs are supposed to be unique identifiers of Australian businesses. The tax office uses them to track and audit how much tax businesses are supposed to pay…The Black Economy Taskforce released an interim report in March that recommends, among other things, the government consider a system to validate ABNs in real time…"

Are your business accounts up to date and accurate?

Having accurate and up-to-date information is critical for business owners to monitor their business activities, make adjustments and plan their tax to maximise legally entitled tax deductions.

It is important to have a regular review and update of your business accounts ensuring that the entries are posted to the correct account, and that tax invoices from suppliers and business sales invoices have correct information and GST amounts.

As you know, taxes are created today and not when the annual financial statements and tax returns are lodged. To legally claim your maximum entitlements and deductions means you need to be proactively planning in advance and make adjustments to business activities to consider taxation and asset protection throughout the year. Do not leave your tax planning to the last minute or the end of the financial year.

The same is true for individuals. Consider tax planning as an important part of life for asset protection.

"It is unwise spending on business assets and money for the sake of claiming tax deductions."

Some business owners and taxpayers mistake tax deductions for tax offset. Both tax deductions and tax offset are related to income tax and income tax legislation in Australian legislation. The main difference is that a tax offset is a lot better than a tax deduction because it can reduce your tax payable to zero; it can't give you a refund if you don't have tax payable. Tax deductions reduce your taxable income and therefore reduce the amount of tax you pay. Expenses can be classified into immediate deductions, not tax deductible, capital expenses, and depreciation expenses by tax laws.

To make this tax law clearer let's look at the following situations:

Tax offset situation:

Tax on income	=	$700.00
Tax offset	=	$1000.00
Outcome Tax payable	=	$0.00

In this case, $1 tax offset reduce $1 tax payable, disregarding your taxable income amount regardless of whether you have a small income or in the millions.

Tax deduction situation:

Income	=	$100,000.00
Expenses	=	$ 99,000.00
Taxable income	=	$ 1,000.00
Tax rate (assumed 30%	=	30%
Tax on income	=	$ 300.00

In this case, you will need to spend $1000.00 immediately on expenses by tax law terminology to save you $300.00 tax. You will find yourself paying $1 to save 30 cents in tax depending on your tax rate. No income means no tax.

It is unwise, and you must avoid spending money on purchasing assets and other unnecessary expenses in order to claim a tax deduction and reduce business profit to little or nil. There are many disadvantages with this approach: the cash flow issue, it makes it difficult to obtain a loan for your business (or a personal loan) and may alert the ATO for an audit because your business is outside the benchmark, etc.

Nineteen top tax planning strategies

Australia's tax legislation is complex and some legislation is constantly changing. Here is a list of tax tips, and planning strategies for Australian Small Business Entity (SBE) taxpayers

1. **Business start-up costs**

   Start-up costs in relation to a proposed business include accountant and lawyer fees for advice relating to business structures or the operation of the business, the setup cost, and underwriting and prospectus fees.

   Claiming tax deductions for business start-up costs requires that the business (taxpayer) is carrying on business in an appropriate manner and is considered as a small business entity according to the tax laws.

2. **Instant asset write-off and depreciation**

   SBE taxpayers can apply a simplified depreciation rule to simplify depreciation for small businesses. This allows the SBE taxpayer to claim an immediate deduction for some assets within the threshold (instant asset write-off) which is a great benefit in reducing taxable income. In order to be qualified for a claim, the asset is either 'used' or 'installed ready for use' in the relevant financial year. Only claim the percentage related to the business.

3. **General SBE pool**

   An SBE taxpayer using simplified depreciation can add an asset above the immediately written-off threshold in to the general small business pool. In order to be qualified for a claim, the asset is either 'used' or 'installed ready for use' in the relevant financial year. Only claim the percentage related to the business.

4. **Accruals expenses vs cash expenses**

   An SBE taxpayer using the accruals accounting method can declare income when sales invoices are issued, and can claim expenses as they are incurred, although they have not been paid yet, including salary, director's fees, rent, etc.

   An SBE taxpayer using the cash accounting method can claim expenses when paid and declare revenue when received.

Be careful about changing the method you use when it comes time to prepare your tax returns, because it may create complications and involve other tax laws.

5. **Deferring income**
   SBE taxpayers using the accrual accounting method who issue invoices need to declare the revenue even though payment has not been received. An SBE taxpayer with a strong cash flow position may consider deferring income and GST by not issuing invoices of the pre-30 June sales, excluding the income and therefore GST for the current financial year. However, the customers might want to receive their invoices for tax deduction purpose.

6. **Accounting for GST in your business – accrual vs cash accounting**
   SBE taxpayers using accrual accounting method in their GST business activities need to report GST when SBE taxpayers issue invoices and when they receive invoices from suppliers.

   SBE taxpayers using the GST cash accounting method only need to declare income when they receive the payment and claim back GST when they pay supplies' invoices.

   GST cash accounting helps to improve SBE taxpayers' cash flow.

7. **Prepayment**

    Prepayment deductions include seminars, airfare and accommodation, subscriptions, rent, phone plans, internet, insurance, leases, advertising and repairs. The prepaid expenses paid by 30 June of a current year are fully deductable in the current financial year and must meet the 12 months rule.

8. **Consumables – three months rule**

    It is important that the SBE taxpayers ensure that purchased consumables, including stationery, are used within three months of the end of the financial year.

9. **Superannuation**

    SBE taxpayers wishing to claim superannuation deductions need to pay superannuation on time. For the last quarter, superannuation needs to be paid before 30 June and received by the superannuation fund before or on 30 June of the relevant financial year.

10. **Trading stock valuation as at 30 June 20xx**

    If your business carries stock, you may need to do a stocktake on the last day of each financial year (30 June 20xx). SBE taxpayers do not need to do stocktake on 30 June if it is estimated that the difference in value of the opening balance on 1 July 20xx and 30 June 20xxx end of year is estimated to be not more than $5,000.

There are three methods that the business taxpayers can use to value the stock at end of financial year:

- Purchase cost
- Market selling value
- Replacement value

Damaged or obsolete stock with no value can be written off to claim a tax deduction.

11. **Scrap assets**

It is a good idea to review your asset ledger and write off all the assets that have been scrapped.

12. **Bad debts**

SBE taxpayers using the accrual accounting method should review trade debtors' accounts and take all possible actions to recover any bad debt prior to write off. See the ATO website for more information.

13. **Donations**

There are a few requirements that need to be met for a donation to be tax deductible

- The organisation/charity has a deductible gift recipient (DGR) endorsement. See the Australian Charities and Not-for-profits Commission (ACNC) website for more information

- It must be a genuine donation, so the taxpayer did not receive benefits such as raffle tickets, gift, food, etc. in return for the donation.
- Taxpayers need to have taxable income to offset the loss. Tax laws do not allow you to claim donations resulting in an additional tax loss.

14. Private use of business assets

It is common that business owners use business assets including motor vehicles for private use, so they need to account for this portion. The private use percentage is not tax deductable and cannot be used to claim GST on expenses.

15. Tax losses

Check your previous year's return for any tax losses carried forward from prior years which you can offset against this year's income if it is passes the tests.

16. Small business entity concessions

SBE taxpayers (trusts, companies, sole traders or partnerships) can access a range of concessions if they are eligible. See the ATO website for more information.

17. Division 7A

Division 7A is a complex piece of legislation. It is one of the high-risk tax areas and the ATO is keeping a close eye on this area. It is best to avoid getting involved with Division 7A where possible to reduce the risk of being audited by the ATO. Here is a suggestion from the ATO:

Avoiding issues in the first place
Division 7A dividends may inadvertently arise as a consequence of a failure to keep private expenses separate from company expenses.

To avoid this:
- don't pay private expenses from a company account
- keep proper records for your company that record and explain all transactions, including payments to and receipts from associated trusts and shareholders and their associates
- if you lend money to shareholders or their associates make sure it's on the basis of a written agreement with terms that ensure it's treated as a complying loan – so the loan amount isn't treated as a Division 7A dividend.

18. Business structure

It is importance to have some understanding of business structures because the structure you choose may affect your responsibilities, the tax payable, asset protections and cost. The four most common business structures in Australia are sole trader, company, trust and partnership. A sole trader business is the simplest and costs are minimal to setup, however it does not offer asset protection. If you want asset protection then either select a company or a corporate trustee with a trust structure. Set up costs are a lot more than for a sole trader business structure.

At the start of business, you may select the business structure that best suits you at the time. As your business grows or changes, you may want to change to a different business structure. You can change your business structure throughout the life of your business, however, this may impact on the cost, ownership of assets, asset protection, etc.

If you are not sure which business structure is best for your business and for you, it is best to seek advice from qualified tax professionals or commercial lawyers. This may cost you several hundred dollars for the advices but it can save you from making costly mistakes and headaches in the future.

19. **ATO benchmarks**

ATO benchmarks is a tool for comparing Small Business Entity (SBE) taxpayer's business performance to other similar businesses in the same industry. There may be a number of reasons why businesses are significantly above or below benchmarks. These include if they are a start-up business, a closing business, bookkeeping into incorrect accounts, tax return declarations for incorrect items, not reporting some expenses, not reporting some income, higher costs, lower selling prices, etc. If you find that there is a mistake, take action to correct it, such as amending your business activity statement or tax return. When the business is significantly above or below ATO benchmarks this may still mean the information is correct as well and there is nothing wrong with the business. However, this may alert the ATO to contact you for more information or conduct an audit.

The ATO uses the information from benchmarks as an indicator in identifying whether businesses may be operating under a cash economy or black economy to avoid paying tax. The information obtained from the benchmarks and data matching allows the ATO to further take action including requesting taxpayers provide more information, a review or audit.

The ATO checks that taxpayers pay the right amount of tax to keep the system fair for all taxpayers and protect honest taxpayers. In addition, the tax collected benefits all Australians and contributes towards the health system, education, transportation and community services.

According to the ATO website:

Our benchmark methodology has been verified as statistically valid by an independent organisation and is consistent with international approaches.

Our benchmarks:

- are based on the biggest data set available – calculated from tax returns and activity statements from over 1.5 million small businesses
- account for businesses with different turnover ranges (up to $15 million) across more than 100 industries
- are published as a range to recognise the variations that occur between businesses due to factors such as location and businesses circumstances.

An ATO benchmark ratio case taken from the ATO website:

Applying a benchmark ratio where there's a lack of records
We identified a computer retail business that was outside of the small business benchmarks along with other risks identified, using our data analysis modelling.

The 'cost of sales to turnover' benchmark for a business in the computer retailing industry with a turnover of $200,001 to $600,000 per annum was 46% to 59% for the year being looked at. This business was reporting at 88% to 96% over a 3-year period. When asked, the business owner couldn't explain why they were reporting so far outside the benchmarks and had few reliable business records to substantiate amounts lodged.

As the business didn't have evidence of their sales, purchases and other records, we decided to apply the benchmark ratio in line with our findings. This resulted in the business having to pay just under $110,000 in tax and more than $27,000 in penalties.

Some ATO data-matching cases taken from the ATO website:
Our ability to match and use data is very sophisticated ...collect information from a number of sources, including banks, other government agencies and industry suppliers...information about purchases of major items, such as cars and real property.

We compare this information against income and expenditure that businesses and individuals have reported to us.

We identify businesses that:
- have told us they no longer operate when they still are
- we think are operating outside of the system
- are cash-only, or mainly deal in cash transactions
- under-report their real income

Example: Unrealistic personal income leads to unreported

millions

The income reported on their personal tax returns indicated that a couple operating a property development company didn't seem to have sufficient income to cover their living expenses.

We found their company had failed to report millions of dollars from the sale of properties over a number of years. A large portion of unreported income had been lost through gambling and significant funds had been sent to an overseas bank account. The couple and their related companies had evaded paying tax of more than $4.5 million.

They had to pay the correct amount of tax based on their income and all their related companies. They also incurred penalties, including:

- administrative penalties (from the tax assessed on the returns that hadn't been lodged – a minimum of 75% of the tax assessed)
- false and misleading statement penalties (because of their intentional disregard of their tax obligations and lack of cooperation during the audit – up to 75% of the shortfall of tax on the returns adjusted to their true income).

Example: Data matching uncovers hidden income

A Melbourne restaurant owner was found to have discrepancies between the business's reported income and the data we received from their bank.

The owner was given the opportunity to let us know if they had made any errors before we started an audit. They consulted their bank and tax agent and advised that the business had failed to report their entire turnover.

Following discussions, the business owner made a voluntary disclosure correcting the business's tax returns for three financial years, resulting in unpaid tax of over $750,000. We accepted this as reasonable because, based on the small business benchmarks, it was equivalent to other businesses in the same industry with the same turnover range.

Example: Failing to report online sales

A Nowra court convicted the owner of a computer sales and repair business on eight charges of understating the business's GST and income tax liabilities.

We investigated discrepancies between income reported by the business and amounts deposited in the business owner's bank accounts. We found the business failed to report income from online sales.

The court ordered the business owner to pay over $36,000 in

unreported tax and more than $18,400 in penalties. The owner was also fined $4,000 and now has a criminal conviction.

CHAPTER 4

CREATING AND KEEPING CUSTOMERS AND CLIENTS FOR LIFE

It is important to study your target market to see whether there is a market for your services and products. You may have a fantastic service or product that would benefit the public, but you can't have a business without customers."

CHAPTER 4

CREATING AND KEEPING CUSTOMERS AND CLIENTS FOR LIFE

The importance of cash and marketing:

> *"When someone stops advertising, someone stops buying. When someone stops buying, someone stops selling. When someone stops selling, someone stops making. When someone stops making, someone stops earning. When someone stops earning, someone stops buying. (Think it over.)"*
> **Edwin H. Stuart**

> *"We [often] have fine theories, but, somehow, we are not always able to carry them out in this workaday world. A chief executive, for example, can draw up a perfect organization chart-and then he wonders why it doesn't function smoothly in practice...If even a Tiffany watch cannot be guaranteed to keep correct time when put to the test of everyday wear and tear, must we not be prepared to make allowance for erring mortals? It is right that executives should draw up perfect plans on paper, but it is all wrong for them to expect their paper plans to work out to perfection in this imperfect world."*
> **B.C Forbes**

How to decide the right products or services to sell

It is critical to have the right products or services at the time to sell to your customers and clients. This is a big contributing factor to having a successful business. Currently, there are tons of products and services offered to customers worldwide, so it is important that you must take a proactive, honest and innovative approach, and review products or services on a regular basis to ensure that you always have the right products or services all the time to sell to the right customers and clients. The right products or services for sale today may not be suitable in three, five and ten years' time to sell, for various reasons including technology changes, or the use of better and different products or services.

"You have got listen to your target market and know your numbers."

Here are 9 most powerful questions you should asking yourself and your team to avoid painful and costly mistakes. You need to analysis your products or services, understand the reasons and customers' buying trigger points, and understand the financial benefit to ensure you make a profit.

1. What are the benefits of using your products or services?
2. Who are the customers buying this products or services?
3. Is this the product or service you want to sell?
4. Is there a demand for the products or services you want to sell to make a profit?

5. What is involved in making the products or services? Are there rules and regulations?
6. What is the return on investment?
7. Why should consumers buy from you instead of your competitors?
8. Do you have enough money to operate the business?
9. Do you have proven systems and processes to attract an ongoing stream of customers?

For a business to be in business it needs to have the products or services to succeed, it must have the right products or right services for the right market, it must sell at the right time and at the right price.

Data from Tradingeconomics.com's Australia Bankruptcies:

Bankruptcies in Australia increased to 846 Companies in July from 708 Companies in June of 2019. Bankruptcies in Australia averaged 672.28 Companies from 1999 until 2019, reaching an all-time high of 1123 Companies in February of 2012 and a record low of 217 Companies in January of 1999.

It is wise to have several products and services to reduce your risk and to implement risk diversification, which involves spreading the risks to a number of areas so any potential impact of a possible negative outcome is limited. This helps to protect your business financial position and reputation. For example, online stores selling goods need to reduce their business risk, because most sellers are selling the same products at a similar price. The secret is to buy quality products at a lower price than your competitors and sell at a similar price to others. In some businesses it is not what you know, it is whom you know that gives you the competitive edge.

As the business owners' goals change, they may add or remove some of the services and products. For example, you may want to combine services that clients need throughout the year and some services that are seasonal, so that you have a regular income streaming throughout the year to ensure that you are still in business in the future.

CHAPTER 5

CREATING A MASSIVE BANK ACCOUNT

"Money is an important success symbol in our culture. Successful people surround themselves with success symbols – positive, pragmatic and supportive examples of solid accomplishment."

Whitt N. Schutz

CHAPTER 5

CREATING A MASSIVE BANK ACCOUNT

> *"Money is a terrible master but an excellent servant."*
> **P. T. Barnum**

How often do you actually set goals and take actions to create a massive bank account?

Journalgazette.net's "New Year's resolution: Fatten your bank account" indicated that while 8 out of 10 Americans had a financial New Year's resolution, 68% of Americans in 2018 had unforeseen financial difficulties. The top three areas were transportation issues, medical care bills and paying off debt.

"Cash is the king and marketing is the queen of business."

Revenue and net profit

I recommended it is best to use software that includes business insight charts of your revenues, expenses, net profit, top ten expenses, top revenue, etc. You may pay extra for the subscription but it will save you thousands of dollars and increase your bottom-line, because you can use the information to generate more sales and cut back on unnecessary expenses. This saves you hours as it only takes a few minutes to analyse the financial position of your business, so you can make decisions and take actions towards your business goals.

"Net profit is more important than revenue generation."

Here are two major assumptions/mistakes I see in both business owners and investors:

Case 1:
The business is growing rapidly and the business owner is very happy that the revenue keeps going up, but the net profit is in red. They did not look at it right. The reality is that the business is losing money.

Case 2:
A company is winning several government tenders, so the assumption is that they must be doing very well with their business. However, the share price of the company keeps dropping over the years with each tender they accept.

Marketing, referrals and pricing are the fast track to create a massive bank account

Marketing increases sales and revenue. It may cost some money, but the return on investment with the right marketing strategies means it will pay for itself many times over. Be creative with your marketing promotion deals:

One of the Coles promotions in 2019: "Collect 10,000 BONUS POINTS or $50 off your shop when you spend $60 or more each week for 4 weeks!"

"Buy 3 tyres and get the 4th free"
"Kids eat free."
Officeworks Price-match Guarantee by 5%
Spend $200 to go into a draw to win a weekend away

Here are more examples from Thebodyfollows.com's "11 Ways to Fatten Your Bank Account with Advertising Boost."

"Upgrade your service and receive a free resort stay in Vegas"
"Spend $100 or more and we will pay for your Orlando hotel!"
"Purchase any three items and get 3 nights in Daytona Beach."
"Sign up for my Webinar and I will comp your 5 Night stay in Cancun."
"Three nights in Branson on me just for attending my open house."
"Refer 3 people to me and your stay in Myrtle Beach is on me."

"Spend just $1 of the $100 voucher and get $15 off your bill!"

Referrals

Referrals are a great way to get clients at low or nil cost. Just keep in mind that it is more likely that your new client is similar to your referrer. For example, if your Class A client referred you a client then it is more likely that your new client is also Class A.

Pricing

Pricing will be covered in more detail in another chapter.

A small increase in fees can result in massive net profit depending on a number of factors including the amount of the purchase, the number of purchases per year and number of customers you have.

For example:

Price increase by	$	10
No. of purchase per year		12
Total extra income /increase	$	120
No. of customers	$	300
Total extra income	$ 36,000	

What will you do with this extra $ 36,000.00?

Here are a few options, you can use it to pay off bills for a stress free lifestyle, invest it back into marketing to get more sales and cash, buy plant and equipment, go overseas for a holiday, pay off your mortgage or give it away.

Here is a list that you may want to start right now:

Goal setting
Marketing action plan
Business action plan
Personal action plan

Have systems for
Tracking your personal income and expenses
Tracking your business income and expenses
Listing rewards as you achieve your goals

CHAPTER 6

STOP DREAMING, START BUILDING THE RIGHT TEAM AND CULTURE

CHAPTER 6

STOP DREAMING, START BUILDING THE RIGHT TEAM AND CULTURE

Businesses may need a business premises, some capital to fund it, an entrepreneur and a team. Many people go into business as individuals, not as a team, and they don't seek advisers to assist them achieve success in both their personal and business life. You can be a sole director of the business, but still seek help from other experts. The other great advantages of having the right team are that you can leverage their time, their expertise, plant and equipment, and many more benefits. The team of people to help with your business may include professional advisors, mentors, staff and others.

Thefreedictionary.com's "Team" definitions including

TEAM = Time, Energy and Money

TEAM = Together Everyone Achieves More

TEAM = Together Everyone Accomplishes More

TEAM = Together Each Achieves More

TEAM = Total Employee Assistance and Management, Inc.

TEAM = Test, Evaluation, Analysis and Modelling

Working with professional advisors and mentors

> *"Many receive advice, only the wise profit by it."*
> **Publilius Syrus**

Seeking professional advice is a vital part of any business, whether you're starting a new one or growing an existing business. Professional advisers may include financial advisers, legal experts, tax advisors, accountants, bankers, and insurance brokers. You use the service of an advisor to get a specific outcome

> *"Not all advisors are the same.*
> *Not all mentors are the same. Usually every mentor*
> *has a mentor."*

Advisors and mentors will have collected tips and strategies that have been proven to work across industries and in various businesses, which they will share with you. You can rely on their advice, which will help you to apply strategies to speed up your business success, and minimise and possibly prevent unnecessary and costly mistakes.

According to Entrepreneur.com's "7 Reasons you need a mentor for entrepreneurial success," Facebook CEO Mark Zuckerberg's mentor was Steve Jobs; Steve Jobs's mentor was Mike Markkula (an early investor and executive at Apple); and Eric Schmidt's mentors were Larry Page and Sergey Brin of Google.

Here is a list of reasons why you want to use the services of various professional advisors or mentors, to:

- Help to clarify your goals, focus on what you need to do, and find the best strategies for achieving those goals
- Hold you accountable
- Gain real life experience which is not found in books
- Help to simplify your business life
- Help to move you in the right direction to prevent making costly mistakes
- Find network opportunities
- Act as trusted advisers
- Help you to have a successful life
- Help you to accomplish your business goals
- Negotiate contracts and other complex documents
- Help you understand and comply with rules and regulations
- Minimise or prevent risk in your business
- Assist in asset protection
- Guide you in tax planning
- Create terms and conditions for your business
- Grow a profitable business

How to find the right advisor or mentor?

Before you look for an advisor, you need to understand your business situation, and figure out what areas you may need advice in. You also need to know your budget. Once you know what kind of advisor you need, find the advisor that has the right skills and experience for your specific needs. You may want an advisor who has some of the characteristics below:

- Continues to invest in self-education
- Continues professional education in their field of expertise.
- Has their own mentor
- Joins the relevant industry associations
- Asks you questions about your specific situation
- Willing to share and teach you about the relevant regulations and laws which relate to your industry
- Has your best interests at heart

Team

> *"As soon as a man climbs up to a high position, he must train his subordinates and trust them. They must relieve him of all small matters. He must be set free to think, to travel, to plan, to see important customers, to make improvements, to do all the big jobs of Leadership."*
> **Herbert N. Casson**

> *"The character and qualifications of the leader are reflected in the men he selects, develops and gathers around him. Show me the leader and I will know his men. Show me the men and I will know their leader. Therefore, to have loyal, efficient employees- be a loyal and efficient employer."*
> **Arthur W. Newcomb.**

When hiring people including employees you may want to consider the following:

- Know who shares your business vision in three to five years' time
- Look for someone who is matched in culture, someone who is competent and capable
- Understand some staff are smarter than you
- Sign off on agreements and expectations early and often so there is no assumptions or misunderstandings
- Train your staff
- Understand and follow the relevant laws including payroll laws when hiring an employee and when letting an employee go

There are many ways people hire staff, but there is no guarantee that you hire the right staff. Even if you think you have hired the right staff in the beginning, the culture may not be suitable for that type of individual. Here are a number of hiring staff processes:

1. **Resume**

   The old fashioned way of hiring people based on their resume and face to face interview. Some companies require applicants to do a fitness test and provide a police clearance document.

2. **Recruitment agencies**

   Some companies prefer to use recruitment agencies to help them find the right staff. The applicants have an interview and may need to complete psychology and skill tests online.

3. **Qualification, skill sets and culture**

   Some big companies go to extreme lengths and use expensive processes to find the right employee. One of my friends had an interview with a large interstate company. They had an interview over the phone then they paid for her flight and accommodation interstate for a second tougher interview. When she arrived for the interview, she was shocked to find that the room was full of people who were similar in age to her and they were also applying for the same position. The job applicants were divided into groups and given a project to complete over the next few days while the employer watched how each applicant performed, working under pressure and interacting with others. She got the job.

4. **Qualification, skill sets and star sign compatibility**

   Several years ago, my friend asked me go with her to a real estate agent. I commented on the pleasant atmosphere of the place, harmony, energy, and a very creative rope type of knot that held many business cards together. The business owner said that in the past they had staff conflict so she changed her strategies when hiring staff including qualification, skill sets and star sign compatibility as part of the criteria for employee selection. This worked out well and now they have a very happy team.

5. **Qualification and skill set for the job**

   Some companies hire employees based on what's worked for them time after time. For example, a manufacturer employs more staff from a particular university than other universities because that particular university is well known for providing the right skill sets and qualifications which match the job requirements, and this is also evident in the staff they hired in the past.

6. **Top student**

   I still remember the proud and extremely happy face of the business owner when he introduced his newly graduated employee as a top mark student from a top university. A few months later this new employee showed me a long list of emails she received from the business owner, because she wanted to know if I also received any emails from the boss. I told her I didn't, and I was very happy that I did not get the emails she showed me. Not long after, she disappeared without a goodbye, so I asked the manager but he walked away to avoid answering my question. The lesson I learned is that a top mark student does not always mean they will be the top performers in your company.

7.   Referral from existing employee

A family and group culture environment allows for hiring staff based on referrals from existing staff. There is zero or low cost, and minimal time required for hiring employees. In this kind of environment there are groups of family, extended family and friends. Some groups have a mother, daughter, uncle and friends working in the same department and in other departments as well. As you know, groups look after each member's interest and they have their own politics, resulting in a very reactive, competitive workplace with lots of issues. It is a great place for people who want to learn the psychology of human behaviour, but it is a nightmare place to work in and almost impossible for an individual not being part of any group, to stand alone, and not be impacted by the politics.

8. Company policy

Some companies have policies in place stating that spouse and family members can't work in the same department or same company to avoid conflicts of interest and for reasons of confidentiality. This means that if an employee happens to meet their spouse at work, one of them has to leave the company.

9. Five-minute interview

Very simple and quick process, as little as a five-minute interview and the employee is offered the job.

10. Interview and practical skills

The applicant has an interview followed by solving a problem. For example the employer hires a qualified bookkeeper. They call the applicant for an interview and then ask them to do some bookkeeping and prepare a Business Activity Statement. This approach will eliminate a number of applicants who are great at the interview stage but not right for the job requirements. You narrow down the right person based on their knowledge and practical skills.

Some businesses use a combination of strategies to hire staff, including advertising, recruitment companies and referrals. As you can see there is no right or wrong way to hire the right employee and it can be a very costly and time-consuming process. The important thing is once you find the right person for the job, you need to keep them happy so that they want to stay with your company. Employers need good systems and processes in place for training staff, promotion, rewarding them and assisting them in achieving their professional and personal goals.

Culture

Culture is the invisible thread that can make-or-break a business. There is a lot to learn from the different cultures that great companies have built. You can live by their culture to build great companies. This is a short cut to help you have an open mind and heart to create the right culture for your business.

Some business owners and management teams overlook the significant risks and impact culture has on customers, staff and business outcomes.

What is culture?

> *"The most distinctive mark of a cultured mind is the ability to take another's point of view;*
> *to put one's self in another's place, and see life and its problems from a point of view different from one's own. To be willing to test a new idea; to be able to live on the edge of difference in all matters intellectually; to examine without heat the burning question of the day; to have imaginative sympathy, openness and flexibility of mind, steadiness and poise of feeling, cool calmness of judgement, is to have culture."*
>
> **Arthur H. R. Fairchild**

> *"Culture is the sum of all the forms of art, of love and of thoughts, which, in the course of centuries, have enabled man to be less enslaved."*
>
> **Andre Malraux**

Referralcandy.com's "Built, not bought: 25 examples of great company culture (2017 update!)" lists:

1. **Southwest Airlines**

   Southwest Airlines reinforce the culture of "Warrior Spirit; Servant's Heart, Fun-loving Attitude".

2. Zappos

All employee including accountant, lawyer, and software developer work in the Call Centre answering calls from customers for the first month. At the end of the training founder and CEO Tony Hsieh will make an offer to pay new employee $2,000 to leave the company immediately. The reason for this is because he does not want to hire staff that are at work for money purpose only.

3. Dropbox

Ferdowsi and Houston know their employees strength, and give them the responsibility to solve problems and being creative as the same time.

4. Twilio

The company focus in innovation, so they expect their new employees must be able to create an app using the company's API.

5. Moz

Rand Fishkin is the founder and CEO of the company is very open and honest in both his personal life and business life including personal finances and disclosed his unsuccessful bid to close the $24m VC deal in 2011.

6. **T/Maker's Heidi Roizen**

Co-founder and CEO Heidi Roizen takes a stand on ethics by being honest and informed their landlord about the inventory that was destroyed in a sprinkler accident. He believes in "How you act – and how you reward or punish the actions of others – will determine how everyone else in the company will act. And that in turn will set the culture – honest or cheating, respectful or disrespectful, friendly or mean, trusting or distrustful"

7. **SumAll and Buffer**

SumAll and Buffer believe in employees' remuneration transparency including employees know the salary of other employees, board meeting for everyone to attend and disclosure the staff salary formula.

8. **Evernote**

Libin hires people based on their strong communication skills: "We want you to be able to explain what you mean we want you to be articulate. That cuts out a lot of people, because a lot of people are probably pretty good technically, but if you don't have excellent communication skills it's going to be very frustrating for you and for other people."

9. Birchbox

Co-founder Katia Beauchamp is very serious about having a positive outlook go-getter attitude. Job applicants who express negative comments and have no direction will not have a chance in getting a job in the company: "If somebody is negative at all about anything, it's done for me. If they describe a past job as not fun, I am literally done because it's your job to make your life fun, and it's in your hands. If you didn't figure out how to make something of it, you're not going to figure out how to make something of it here."

10. Medium

Medium has a number of experimental interview process and validation to discover that "Teach me something" is the best way to selecting the right candidate.

11. Twitter

Twitter commits to providing employees ongoing training and a quarterly Hack Week to explore and obtain maximum benefits from employees' ideas.

12. Costco

CEO Craig Jelinek wrote to Congress requesting to increase the minimum wage: "We know it's a lot more profitable in the long term to minimize employee turnover and maximize employee productivity, commitment and loyalty."

13. Continental

Continental stands by their employees, and believe that the customer is not always right. The former CEO has let go of an unreasonable customer – "Dear Mrs Crabapple, we will miss you. Love, Herb."

14. Etsy

Etsy offered a $5,000 grant to each young woman engineer who enrols in Hacker School and therefore received a considerable number of female applicants from 7 to 51. This assists in building a rising star team.

15. Treehouse

CEO Ryan Carson realised that he is exhausted from continually working long hours, but the productivity is not optimised. He changes both his working habit and his employee number of work day per week from working long hours to four hard day work week in order to optimise productivity and have a work-life balance.

16. Shopify

Deloitte's research data shows the important of peer recognition increase as much as 14% staff engagement and productivity. Shopify has advantage of this finding by creating an internal tool (UNICORN) so the employees can praise each other for a job well done and give each other cash bonuses option: "When we hit 20,000 followers on Twitter, someone noticed and posted a message on UNICORN thanking our social media manager. Right away, there were high fives in the hallways and the person responsible was walking around with a huge smile on her face."

17. Warby Parker

Warby Parker is proactively constantly improving company culture by having a culture team responsible for planning company outings, themed luncheons, and events.

18. Adobe

Adobe allows managers acting as coaches which helps to motivate employee to be creative and innovative.

19. Quora

At Quora a new employee learns from mentors and other employees all the time.

20. Morning Star

Morning Star is a world leading tomato processor. Morning Star has no actual human managers that employees have to follow. Morning Star's "boss" is the Morning Star mission that all employees follow. The company expect every employee to create their personal mission statement detailing their contribution to Morning Star mission and expect employee to achieve it. There is self-management institute white papers.

21. NextJump

NextJump looks after staff wellbeing by having a gym for employees and take a step further by encourage the employee to be part of the program where the company creates teams to compete against one another requiring all employees to record their work-out in the computer. The winner is the employee who has worked-out the most for the week to win $1000 each week.

22. Scripps

Scripps is a healthcare company and committed to provide employee wellbeing including doctors on demand, medical coverage, free food, on-site massage therapy and employee's pet insurance to reduce employee stress when their pet is not well.

23. Patagonia

Patagonia wants their employee trust in the product they sell, so the company policy since 1973, "let my people go surfing …Other than helping to refresh the mind, encouraging employees to leave the office for outdoor activities fosters a strong belief in the product they're selling with employees being encouraged to test out their apparel regularly. If an employee really believes in the product, it will come across to the client."

24. Atlassian

Shipit Days (four days a year) are creative days working on their creative project, not normal routine work.

25. Whole Foods

Employees get 20% discount on purchases but up to 30% discount if the employee stays healthy and meets criteria for blood pressure, cholesterol, smoking status and body-mass-index (BMI) screenings and there is a website for employee to keep track of their eating habits.

CHAPTER 7

PROCRASTINATION

CHAPTER 7

PROCRASTINATION

"When duty calls me, I'm prepared
As though our goals were aimed and shared.
I draw my breath in, shoulders straight,
And quietly procrastinate."
Alison W Birch

You are not alone with procrastination. Everyone, including famous people, procrastinate at some time in their life and may put themselves under pressure to complete goals or live to regret missed opportunities. Psychologytoday.com's "Procrastination: Ten Things To Know" found 20% of people identify themselves as chronic procrastinators. Some common situations people procrastinate before doing:

- Lodge income tax returns
- Lodge Business Activity Statements
- Last minute gift shopping for birthday, anniversary and Christmas
- Study for exam
- Chores
- Lose weight

- Quit smoking
- Reduce alcohol intake
- Exercise
- Go back to study
- Change career
- Start a business
- Visit dentist
- Visit doctor for health check
- Pay bills
- Buy tickets to concerts
- An outing
- Catch up with friends and family
- Buy insurance
- Shop

Procrastination can cause you money problems, relationship breakdown, stress, regret, fear, and make your life unnecessarily unpredictable and complicated.

All through history, some of the most famous people and leaders in the world faced the same issues of procrastination throughout their lives, but they managed to make a name for themselves. The following information is taken from Careeraddict.com's "Top 10 Most Famous Procrastinators in the World", Procrastinus.com's "Procrastination and Science Famous Procrastinators" and some extracts from their biographies.

18 Famous people are procrastinators:

1. Samuel Taylor Coleridge (1875 -1912)

Samuel Taylor Coleridge is well known for his poetry. He had difficulty staying focused when writing due to distractions of other things, so his writing is brief. His most loved work, 'Kubla Khan' is incomplete.

> "Readers may be divided into four classes: 1) Sponges, who absorb all that they read and return it in nearly the same state, only a little dirtied. 2) Sand-glasses, who retain nothing and are content to get through a book for the sake of getting through in time. 3) Strain-bags, who retain merely the dregs of what they read. 4) Mogul diamonds, equally rare and valuable, who profit by what they read, and enable others to profit by it also."
>
> **Samuel Taylor Coleridge**

2. Margaret Atwood (1939–)

Margaret Atwood is an author whose work includes fourteen novels, nine short story collections and sixteen poetry books, articles and short works. She allows herself to procrastinate to 3pm because she works best in the afternoon.

> *"If you feel that there's the author and then the character, then the book is not working. People have a habit of identifying the author with the narrator, and you can't, obviously, be all of the narrators in all of your books, or else you'd be a very strange person indeed."*
> **Margaret Atwood**

3. Truman Capote (1924–1984)

Truman Capote was one of the best writers in the world. He is an American author, artist and actor. Unfortunately he never managed to complete his masterpiece – *Answered Prayers*. He was even offer a $1million cheque for him to complete it. Four chapters were published in *Esquire* magazine, but he died before it was complete. People were disappointed.

> *"Love, having no geography, knows no boundaries."*
> **Truman Capote**

4. Leonardo Da Vinci (1452–1519)

Leonardo Da Vinci's masterpieces include the *Mona Lisa*, *The Last Supper* and *Vitruvian Man*. *Mona Lisa* took him 16 years to complete, *Virgin of the Rocks* took more than 13 years to complete, and he had a number of uncompleted projects, due to his procrastination and lack of focus.

> *"Life is pretty simple: You do some stuff. Most fails. Some works. You do more of what works. If it works big, others quickly copy it. Then you do something else. The trick is the doing something else. "*
> **Leonardo da Vinci**

5. Frank Lloyd Wright (1867–1959)

Frank Lloyd Wright is one of the most famous American architects and designed the beautiful Fallingwater weekend house retreat for Edgar Kauffman's family. Frank procrastinated in drawing up the building plans until a few hours prior to the meeting.

> *"Architecture is the triumph of human imagination over materials, methods, and men, to put man into possession of his own Earth. It is at least the geometric pattern of things, of life, of the human and social world. It is at best that magic framework of reality that we sometimes touch upon when we use the word order."*
> **Frank Lloyd Wright**

6. Saint Augustine (354–430)

Saint Augustine of Hippo was a serious procrastinator. He found it hard for him to commit to his holy path and overcome his temptations. However, Augustine came across one of Paul's letters from the Bible which motivated him to return to his holy path. He became a Saint Augustine later in life.

> *"Take care of your body as if you were going to live forever; and take care of your soul as if you were going to die tomorrow."*
> **Saint Augustine**

7. Franz Kafka (1883–1924)

Franz Kafka wrote about the human struggle for communication and self-doubt in novels including *Amerika*, *The Trial* and *The Castle*. These books were published because his friend Max Brod did not follow his request to destroy any unpublished manuscripts. Brod also published other Kafka stories as well.

> *"If I shall exist eternally, how shall I exist tomorrow?"*
> **Frank Kafka**

8. **Victor Hugo (1802–1885)**

   Victor Hugo was a French poet, novelist and dramatist. His masterpieces are *Les Miserables* and *The Hunchback of Notre Dame*. He had a unique way to stop procrastination and to get on with his work by asking his servant to remove all his clothes and leave him naked in his study room and not gave back his clothes until a scheduled hour.

   > *"He, who every morning plans the transactions of the day, and follows that plan, carries a thread that will guide him through a labyrinth of the most busy life."*
   > **Victor Hugo**

9. **Bill Clinton (1946–)**

   Bill Clinton was the 42nd president of United States from 1993 to 2001. It was a challenge to keep Bill to schedules and he did things at the last minute.

   > *"From a Bill Clinton speech: 'People are more impressed by the power of our example rather than the example of our power...'"*
   > **Bill Clinton**

10. Dalai Lama (1935–)

Dalai Lama is a great spiritual leader travels the world teaching about compassion and happiness. In the early years of his life he was a procrastinator, leaving everything to the last minute to get work done. However, now he is teaching people his lessons:

> *"You must not procrastinate. Rather, you should make preparations so that even if you did die tonight, you would have no regrets. If you develop an appreciation for the uncertainty and imminence of death, your sense of the importance of using your time wisely will get stronger and stronger."*
>
> **Dalai Lama**

11. Herman Melville (1819–1891)

Herman Melville is one of the greatest American writers and poets. He was procrastinating to complete the great book *Moby-Dick or the Whale*, so to overcome it his wife chained him to the desk to help him complete the book.

> *"As for me, I am tormented with an everlasting itch for things remote. I love to sail forbidden seas, and land on barbarous coasts."*
>
> **Herman Melville**, *Moby-Dick, or, the Whale*

12. Johann Rall (1726–1776)

Johann Rall was a German commander in charge of Hessian troops. On Christmas night in 1776 Johann and his troops were not prepared for attack. They celebrated by getting drunk, playing chess and cards. Johann was totally focused on finishing the card game which became a higher priority than reading a note handed to him by a local loyalist warning him Washington's troops were approaching. Washington's troops attacked the next morning and won the battle of Trenton. Johann was injured and died shortly after. It was discovered later that the note warning about the attack was never read, left unopened in his coat pocket.

13. Gene Fowler (1890–1960)

Gene Fowler was an author of seventeen books and numerous screenplays during his famous career in Hollywood.

> *"Writing is easy. All you do is stare at a blank sheet of paper until drops of blood form on your forehead."*
> **Gene Fowler**

14. Marcus Aurelius (121–180)

Marcus Aurelius was a Roman emperor and Stoic philosopher. He was the last ruler of 'Five Good Emperors'. At the time his empire controlled a majority of the western world. He is well known as a famous non-procrastinator, and this is one of his famous quotes:

> *"Think of all the years passed by in which you said to yourself "I'll do it tomorrow," and how the gods have again and again granted you periods of grace of which you have not availed yourself. It is time to realize that you are a member of the Universe, that you are born of Nature itself, and to know that a limit has been set to your time. Use every moment wisely, to perceive your inner refulgence, or 'twill be gone and nevermore within your reach."*
> **Marcus Aurelius**

15. Samuel Johnson (1709–1784)

Samuel Johnson was an English author and lexicographer. He procrastinated writing articles until the last minute when he was under pressure. He described the word procrastination in one of his weekly magazines *The Rambler*:

> *"One of the general weaknesses, which in spite of the instruction of moralists, and the remonstrances of reason, prevail to a greater or less degree in every mind."*

16. Douglas Adams (1952–2001)

Douglas Adams is one of the authors of *Hitchhiker's Guide to the Galaxy*. He procrastinated and he hated writing, so his publishers and editors locked him in a room and pressured him to complete his work. His other novel was *The Salmon of Doubt*, which had been a work in progress for ten years. He hadn't finished the first draft when he died of a heart attack in 2001.

> *"I love deadlines. I like the whooshing sound they make as they fly by."*
> **Douglas Adams**

17. General George McClellan (1826–1885)

General McClellan was known for his endless preparation of the Union Army and hesitated to take action resulting in missed opportunity when the war was taking longer to end.

> *"Conscious of my own weakness, I can only seek fervently the guidance of the Ruler of the Universe, and, relying on His all-powerful aid, do my best to restore Union and peace to a suffering people, and to establish and guard their liberties and rights."*
> **George B. McClellan**

18. Hamlet

Hamlet is the prince of Demark in Shakespeare's story. It is a tragic story where he is hesitant to take revenge for his murder.

> *"To be, or not to be: that is the question:*
> *Whether 'tis nobler in the mind to suffer*
> *The slings and arrows of outrageous fortune,*
> *Or to take arms against a sea of troubles,*
> *And by opposing end them? To die: to sleep;*
> *No more; and, by a sleep to say we end*
> *The heart-ache and the thousand natural shocks*
> *That flesh is heir to, 'tis a consummation*
> *Devoutly to be wish'd. To die, to sleep;*
> *To sleep: perchance to dream: ay, there's the rub."*
> **- William Shakespeare**, *Hamlet*

Psychologytoday.com's "Procrastination: Ten Things to Know" article mentions that "Procrastinators sabotage themselves. They put obstacles in their own path. They actually choose paths that hurt their performance..."

"The hardest thing to do is take the first step then it is almost done."

Top 7 Actions to overcome procrastination

1. Write a daily action plan.

2. Be determined to complete a certain activity by a certain time.

3. Budget time for distractions including emails, phone calls and people dropping in without notice.

4. Have a default time scheduled for distractions. For example checking emails at 3:30pm.

5. Get up early and start your day full of energy. For example, go for a walk in the bushland, lake area, beach, or coastal area.

6. Have rewards for completed tasks and to relax the mind, such as outings, swimming or going to a café.

7. Don't over-think. If you get stuck, or are undecided, move on and come back later. It's a work in progress - you can perfect it later.

CHAPTER 8

HOW TO MAKE $$$ EFFORTLESSLY WHILE YOU SLEEP

CHAPTER 8

HOW TO MAKE $$$ EFFORTLESSLY WHILE YOU SLEEP

> *"The best customer service is if the customer doesn't need to call you, doesn't need to talk to you. It just works."*
> **Jeff Bezos**

"Is that possible to make money while you're asleep?"

The answer is yes, it is possible to make money while you sleep.

Jeff Bezos is the founder and CEO of Amazon which is the biggest online retailer in the world. Initially Amazon was selling books, but it expanded to including selling other stuff as well.

> *"The framework I found, which made the decision (to start Amazon in 1994) incredibly easy, was what I called a regret minimization framework. I wanted to project myself forward to age 80 and say, 'OK, I'm looking back on my life. I want to minimize the number of regrets I have.' And I knew that when I was 80, I was not going to regret having tried this. I was not going to regret trying to participate in this thing called the Internet that I thought was going to be a really big deal. I knew that if I failed, I wouldn't regret that. But I knew the one thing I might regret is not ever having tried. I knew that that would haunt me every day."*
> **Jeff Bezos.**

> *"When I was in college, I remember thinking to myself, this internet thing is awesome because you can look up anything you want, you can read news, you can download music, you can watch movies, you can find information on Google, you can get reference material on Wikipedia, except the thing that is most important to humans, which is other people, was not there."*
> **Mark Zuckerberg (Facebook CEO)**

Make money effortlessly while you sleep is another term for passive income. In an ideal world making passive money requires little effort and little time to maintain it; money should be automatically arriving in your bank account every month. Most people think of real estate and share trading as passive income. However, there are numerous ways to generate multi-sources of passive income both nationally and internationally.

It is important to continue having a steady stream of income as we are living longer, so we need to earn more financially to support our lifestyle. If you have 30 additional years added to your life, do you have enough cash reserves to live on, how might you carry on with your life?

According to Allianzlife.com' "One-third of Americans regret major life choices, but many embrace newfound opportunity to rechart course." They found:

- 32% of Americans regret the major life decisions and choices they made in their lives including their education and career
- 56% of people would take up more travel to places
- 35% of people would like to live in different location if they live extra 30 years
- 36% of people would like to take more risks with their lives including new jobs, and going back to study
- 39% of people regret that they did not make their dream to reality
- 38% of people regret that they did not take risks with their profession

- 49% of Americans said with the possibility of extra 30 years would completely change their major life decisions, live an ideal lifestyle, take more career breaks, not follow the established traditional life pattern of going to school, get married, have a family then retirement
- 91% of the people agreed that with the prospect of living longer need to think about financial planning

Everyone has the same number of hours in a day and number of days in the year. We have certainty that there are 24 hours in a day, 365 days a year and a leap year is 366 days. Time is very precious. There are always opportunities to make money and the goal is to have regular cash coming into your bank account. However, you need to understand risk management. Money always flows from one person to the next person worldwide. Money never sleeps, no matter what the economy or weather is doing at the time.

There are millions of people who are making money effortlessly while they sleep around the world and it is increasing rapidly. But how? By a combination of having the right information, products and services, the right tools, right people, use of internet and social media, it is a lot easier to make money on line 24/7 at low cost. Here is a list of ideas that have helped others to make lots of money:

1. **Webinars and Seminars**

   Webinars are a wonderful way to make money while you sleep because you only need to record the webinar then you can resell it to endless people to watch for a fee.

2. **Coaching and consulting services**

   There are a number of ways to sell your coaching and consulting services both online and in person including having a website, direct mail, site visits, or you may be able to sell your coaching and consulting services after people watch your webinars.

3. **Online courses**

   Online courses are a great way to earn extra income and require relatively little effort and time in updating the information. Online courses are very popular because people can watch when it suits them. What course can you teach? It is best that the course is about your passion and area of expertise.

4. **Inner circle mastermind group**

   An Inner circle mastermind group is an exclusive group which gives members a competitive edge in a market place. Some of these groups have a limited number of members. Some of the best mastermind groups can cost six figures or more.

5. **Build your database**

   Build your database by offering free sample products or information to subscribers first. Some of these subscribers may end up buying your products and services or affiliate products and services that you are promoting.

6. **Membership site**

   Create a membership site to receive regular membership fees in exchange for your information, advice, training or products.

7. **Website**

   Create a website or a landing page to sell your products and services.

8. **Online store**

   An online store importing goods and selling online is not for everyone. It is a 24/7 store that does not need to have a physical premises, and is open to worldwide customers with no time difference globally. It is not what you know, it is who you know. The internet, the right tools, the right information and the right team will enable you to import quality products according to the rules and regulations of the countries involved. These days you can import and sell products worldwide without seeing the goods, seeing the customers or seeing the money as the funds are automatically transferred and appear in your bank account. The buyers are the ones who get to see the physical products.

9. **Affiliate marketing**

   Affiliate marketing requires you have an email list of people for marketing. If you don't have a list, then you may want to build an email list through Facebook or YouTube.

10. **Others**

    Audio

    Book sales online and in book stores

    Paid blog

    Paid articles

11. **Be a reseller of software**

12. **Share trading**

    Share trading can be a risky investment.

13. **Option trading**

    Options trading can be a very risky investment. I recommend that you seek advice.

14. **Real estate**

    Invest in real estate including residential property or commercial properties to earn rental income, tax benefits and for possible capital growth purposes. You can purchase the property locally, interstate or overseas. I recommend that you seek advice.

15. Cryptocurrencies

Cryptocurrencies are digital assets and are a very volatile and high risk investment.

16. Superannuation investment options

Some of the superannuation funds allow you to decide how you want to invest your superannuation money.

CHAPTER 9

PROFIT, PRICE WAR, AND PRICING STRUCTURE

CHAPTER 9

PROFIT, PRICE WAR, AND PRICING STRUCTURE

> *Several weeks of summer vacation in the Thirties I spent working at $15 a week in the Forbes office... I worked in the mail cage, where envelopes were slit and subscription payments extracted. Dad used to come pounding down the office aisle and pause long enough to ask, "How much today?" Inevitably the answer was inadequate – except once. That day the controller said excitedly, "Mr Forbes, the ledger shows a slight profit this month!"... My father turned to him and said, "Young man, I don't give a damn what your books show. Do we have any money in the bank?"*
>
> **Malcolm Forbes**

Should your business go into a price war?

"It depends on your business goal – low cost structure to build your market share

or

prevent and stop a price war before it begins if possible."

It depends. You will find the answer to this question below. Lets looks at the impact of increased prices and decreased prices on the profit.

The impact of price increases on profit

A relatively small increase in price can have a big impact on the profit depending on the number of customers you have and the amount of money each customer purchases from you each year.

Price increase by	$	10
No. of purchase per year		12
Total extra income /increase	$	120
No. of customers	$	300
Total extra income	$ 36,000	

As you can see from the table below if you increase the price by 20%, you can afford to let go 40% of your sales while maintaining the same 30% gross margin. This means you have less sales, more time, and keep the same % gross margin. The figures in the table below are a combination of information taken from Tim Atterton's Financial Dynamics seminar note, and Hedgescompany.com's "How a price increase or decrease affects gross profit vs unit sales"

Business % Gross profit or % Margin							
10	15	20	25	30	35	40	50
% Price Increase	% sales volume can fall to have the same profit						
2	17	12	9	7	6	5	5	4
3	23	17	13	11	9	8	7	6
5	33	25	20	17	14	12	11	9
10	50	40	33	29	25	22	20	17
15	60	50	43	37	33	30	27	23
20					40	36	33	29

The impact of price discounts on profit

As you can see from the table below using the discounting method to drive more sales into your business by discounting 20% on your price means that you will need to increase your sales volume by 200% in order to keep the same 30% gross profit. This is helpful information to keep in mind when you want to use the discounting method, and be prepared to work a lot harder too. The figures in the table below are taken from various sources including the book called "The 10 Day Turnaround" by Spike Humer & Darren J Stephens, Tim Atterton's "Financial Dynamics" seminar notes, and Hedgescompany.com's "How a price increase or decrease affects gross profit vs unit sales"

Business % Gross profit or % Margin							
10	15	20	25	30	35	40	50
% sales volume must increase to have the same profit							
% Discount							
2	25	15	11	9	7	6	5	4
3	43	25	18	14	11	9	8	6
5	100	50	33	25	20	17	14	11
10		200	100	67	50	40	33	25
15			300	150	100	75	60	43
20				400	200	133	100	67
25					500	250	167	100
30						600	300	150

Some businesses including airlines, retailers, and phone companies have been implementing a number of strategies to get the customers and clients from their competitors. One of the well know strategies is a price war, a tactic where a business advertises cheaper products and services than their competitors, and accepts less net profit in order to keep their customers and get new customers.

Some price war businesses do not make much profit, or they even run at a loss, so they can't afford to provide quality services and product. Price wars hurt a business' bottom line and may lead some businesses to close altogether.

Hbr.org's "How to Flight A Price War" article gives examples of various industries including airlines, telecommunication, E-trade and electronic brokers:

- In 1992 the American Airlines, Northwest Airlines, and other U.S. carriers went on matching fare prices and even exceeding one another's reduced fares resulting in record sales and losses. The only winner is the customers; the bottom line is these airlines are worse off than before they joined the price war battle.

- In July 1999, Sprint promoted off-peak rate night-time long-distance rate at five cents per minute. In August 1999, MCI matched Sprint's promotion special off-peak rate. Later that month AT & T announced that their sales had dropped and decided to join the price war battle by cutting its long-distance rates to 7 cents per minute all day for a month at $5.95. As a result, AT&T's share price dropped 4.7% when the announcement was made, MCI's shares fell 2.5%; Sprint's fell 3.8%.

- Internet enables some businesses to price match their competitors low price including E-Trade and other electronic brokers; as a result some companies' share prices have dropped from $30 to $15 to $8 over the years.

Planning before starting a price war

Discounts, a loyalty program, and bulk-buy pricing are common business practices for:

- Reducing over stock
- Clearing last season's stock or outdated models
- Getting more customers and prospective customers without a massive marketing campaign
- Increasing sales to meet sales target goals during a slow sales season
- Getting free advertising on sales websites
- Generating new sales from new customers and current customers, and persuading inactive customers come back
- Encouraging customers to purchases goods and services especially if the special has a limited time offer

Before you discount, do some planning to work out your offers and your numbers to ensure that you are still making a profit from the extra sales coming in:

- Work out your current profit margin, mark-up and breakeven figures to be able to price cut without making a loss
- Work out the best discount price that allows you to still make extra profit on the sales
- Prepare a marketing plan to get new customers, increase sales from the existing customers, and bring inactive customers back
- Analyse what your competitors are offering and their pricing structure
- Decide on the discounting timeframe
- Constantly review your business's financial data

Don't get involved with price wars in the first place if possible
Price wars are dangerous because they give the illusion that the business is expanding as the revenue is going up, but in reality the business works a lot harder with less profit and in some cases making a loss. The share price of the company may drop in price, you may have to lower the quality standard, outsource overseas and take longer delivery time, etc.

It is important to know your target customers buying decisions – not all customers are after a low price. Some customers select quality over price and are willing to pay extra for a number of reasons including paying more for delivery on time, hassle free service, a guarantee, consistent quality in order to make their business run smoothly, with more customers and more profit.

Hbr.org's "How to Flight A Price War" article mentions some businesses are not interested in getting involved in a price war by having other policies in place and not advertising the following words: price-matching, everyday low pricing, and other public declarations, indicating they do not intend to go into a price war. For example, Food Lion stopped their prices as soon as they heard their competitors were willing to price match their price structure by putting up their prices.

If possible, be one step ahead of your competitors. Price wars often occur within the same industry and sometime from different industries. The time spent analysing your business and other industry competitors including pricing structure, capabilities and positioning is time well invested in ensuring you create the right products and services for the emerging target market. Hbr.org's "How to Flight A Price War" article gives a few examples of how to stop a price war before it begins including Encyclopaedia Britannica, Ritz-Carlton and McDonald's.

- Encyclopaedia Britannica noticed that their encyclopaedia sales had dropped and their finding indicated the main competitor was not Grolier's Encyclopaedia but Microsoft.

This helped Britannica make use of technology and the internet as the way consumers get information has changed. So by providing free access to its database on the web it's able to generate its revenue from banner adverts and not consumers.

- The Ritz-Carlton avoids price wars by being creative, offering a 'technology butler' who can fix laptops and other electronic devices…The Ritz-Carlton also offered a 'bath menu' of drinks and snacks to be served along with butler-drawn baths. Guests who stayed more than five nights received an embroidered pillowcase."

- McDonald's changed customers' perception and choices. "McDonald's… faced Taco Bell's 59-cent taco strategy in the 1980s by bundling burgers, fries, and drinks into value meals… McDonald's reframed the price war from tacos versus burgers to lunch versus lunch."

If you decide to go into a price war make sure that your competitors know that your price is so low that there is no profit for your competitors. Sara Lee has a major advantage over their competitors in that Sara Lee has low variable costs and the products sell at a relatively high price compared with those of its competitors. In the event of a price war and to stop price wars, Sara Lee uses price dropping strategy to a point that its competitors can't profitably match. Sara Lee's management team are very smart in using this strategy to prevent price wars.

Ten ways to increase your business' profit

- **Special offers**

  Special offers can include offering free gift wrapping or free shipping.

- **Package or bundle deal**

  This is an upselling opportunity to encourage and reward customers to purchase more stock or services, by including things like 10% off having a haircut and buying shampoo and conditioner.

- **Bulk buying discounts**

  This technique is a common practice with retailers and some airline industries offering buy one get one half price.

- **Value added offers**

  A value-added offer can help to retain your great customers. A salon can offer a free treatment or blow wave with haircut.

- **Seasonal or periodic discounts**

  Seasonal or periodic discounts throughout the year help boost your revenue and reduce your stocks.

- **Safeguard your assets to prevent theft**

  Have systems in place to keep track of your assets and stop possible money being stolen by employees or customers.

- **Inventory systems**

  Use an electronic inventory system to keep track of your inventory. This will help prevent you from buying extra stock or over-ordering, as well as cash flow issues, while reducing theft and tracking stock obsolescence. The information will help you decide how much stock to purchase and which stocks are making money and selling fast. An electronic inventory system makes it easy to keep track of your stock and you save yourself hours without the need to look up old purchases invoices or do manual stock counts.

- **Check supplier bills**

  Check all invoices to ensure that you have not been overcharged for goods or services you haven't received or been invoiced at the wrong price

- **Increase your prices**

  Every year most of your business running costs are increasing, so you should increase your prices to match your suppliers price rises and also with your competitors' price. See previous table - if you have a margin of 50% and you increase 10% in price it means you can afford to lose 17% of your customers and still maintain the same margin.

- **Pricing structure**

  Reviewing your pricing structure can help with your cash flow, reduce bad debt and increase bottom line.

Reasons why you should quote upfront vs hourly rate

The three most common ways of business quoting and invoicing are: upfront, work in progress and hourly rate. Some businesses use a combination of these methods depending on their clients' circumstances.

1. **Quote upfront**

    This is the best option because there is no bad debt. You can set your goals to achieve your desired hourly rate, get paid for producing results and there are no nasty surprises. Sometimes you may quote correctly, other times you may under-quote or over-quote. You learn from your experience and get better at upfront quoting next time. Sometimes it's impossible to get prepayment from your clients for various reasons including cash flow issues, worry the other people may take their money and not provide the services, their experience with you in the past, and with similar business dealings if it is a work in progress or to be paid on completion. If you want to go down this path make sure that you understand the impact on your business if some of your clients leave you when you change your quoting and invoicing process. It is a good idea to try this out on a small number of your clients to start with. For example, my lawyer quotes upfront and requires payment in their trust account prior to providing advice or carrying out any work. This can be tough on cash flow.

2. Work in progress and charge hourly rate

If your fee is set as an hourly rate then there's a limit to the number of hours that you can work in a day. This method is used by some businesses for a variety of reasons, including that they get used to it, and/or don't know how long it takes to complete the tasks so they are not sure about the final fee they should quote. They can worry about the clients' reaction, and worry they may under-quote if they provide a fixed fee.

The sad thing about this invoicing work in progress method is there is always a risk of bad debt and issues with fees with customers, which may result in voluntarily writing off the fee or involuntarily writing off the fee. The other disadvantage with hourly rate is that as you become more effective and efficiently complete the project, your actual overall rate drops because you bill by the hour.

There are other factors to consider such as how technology and the internet may affect the payment. If hourly rate is your invoicing method, then you may be earning less each day as you get better at providing your service, use better software and utilise better internet.

One way to maintain the same hourly rate as you become more efficient is to increase your chargeable rate and be prepared that some of your clients may complain and leave you for some other provider at a cheaper rate. Another way is to provide a fixed fee.

3. **Combination of upfront and work in progress invoicing**

   Some businesses use a combination of payment methods including upfront payment, work in progress payment and payment on completion, depending on the services required at the time. For example, a tradie may ask for deposits for materials then pay on completion if the project does not take too long to complete. If the project stretches over a period of time, they may use the work in progress approach.

CHAPTER 10

HAVE THE INNER STRENGTH TO BOUNCE BACK WHEN FACED WITH PAINFUL AND COSTLY MISTAKES IN YOUR BUSINESS

"*Will is the master of the world. Those who want something, those who know they want, even those who want nothing, but want it badly, govern the world.*"

Ferdinand Brunetiere

CHAPTER 10

CREATING A MASSIVE BANK ACCOUNT

> *"Achievement seems to be connected with action.*
> *Successful men and women keep moving.*
> *They make mistakes but they don't quit."*
> **Conrad Hilton (founder of Hilton Hotels)**

This chapter contains real life stories of hope and inspiration about my mentor Ian Marsh and a number of famous people worldwide throughout history who have hit rock bottom, and how they found the inner strength to bounce back from painful and expensive experiences once again to make a name for themselves. As you can imagine being broke is tough, stressful and disappointing, which impact on how you view yourself and how others view you, and make you worry about how you can take care of your family, pay staff and pay creditors. We hope that it never happens to us. Most people are not very good at handling failure; failure is the final blow for some people and they give up all their passions and dreams. However, in this chapter we look at a number of businesses and entrepreneurs who never gave up, bounced back from bankruptcy and achieved their greatest successful and financial status once again.

> *"One of the most important things I have learned is that businesses don't fail, entrepreneurs give up. Now sometimes, giving up is the right decision. But usually you just need to dig in and figure out how to make things better. Remember: Every day is a new opportunity to get up and do it better than yesterday."*
> **Adda Birnir**

Time after time, it has proven to me the power of words and the lasting impact on people's life. Words are so powerful that they can make or break your success and relationships, create peace or war, or bring you hope. Here is a quotation and case study proving the power of words has great impact on people's life:

> *"The power of words is immense. A well-chosen word has often sufficed to stop a flying army, to change defeat into victory, and to save an empire."*
> **Emile De Girardin**

Ian Marsh

Here is a real-life story illustrating the impact of Ian's mentor, Mal, whose words have helped him to become a multimillionaire once again within a year, instead of going down the path of broken dreams. According to Streetsmartbusinessschool.com video 'How To Never Be Broke Again!', in the year 2000 Ian was at his lowest point in life. He was busy focusing on expanding his business, then one day he discovered that his staff, who he regarded as his family, actually stole $10 million from his business. Ian had to declare himself bankrupt. The hardest part was to tell his wife that he no longer had the finances to support the family. He flew from Queensland to Perth to say thanks and goodbye to his mentor at the time, Mal Emery. Ian told Mal that this was the last time they would cross paths; he had become bankrupt and couldn't afford to continue the mentoring program. His next goal was to go to Byron Bay, get really drunk and look at the naked women. Mal replied:

"Ok Ian, if that's the case it was nice knowing you, I guess I won't be seeing you again. But I don't think this will be the case! Wake up to yourself you idiot! You just had a ten-million-dollar education. You did it once, you can do it again!"

Ian took Mal's words very seriously. He bounced back full of motivation and gave up one of his bucket list ideas of getting drunk in Byron Bay. He transferred his energy to starting over again and took massive action to build up four more multimillion-dollar businesses.

> *"Most people spend their time going around a problem instead of facing it head on!"*
> **Ian Marsh**

13 Famous people worldwide bounce back from major setbacks

Here are 13 famous people from throughout history that you may have heard of or know of who have gone through extremely tough conditions prior to making a name for themselves.

1. Soichiro Honda (1906–1991)

Soichiro Honda is the founder of Honda automobiles. According to Indiatimes.com's "11 Inspiring stories of people who bounced back after failing" his factory has been destroyed three times: twice by being bombed in World War II and then by an earthquake. He held onto his dreams and manufactured a scooter that was a huge seller on the US market.

> *"[On Napoleon] I imagined him to have a physique as imposing and strong as his reputation merited. When I discovered from reading history books that he was a small man, I was not at all disillusioned. I'm not very big myself, and it was obvious that you don't measure a man's greatness by his physical size, but by his acts, by the impact he makes on human history. I also learned that Napoleon was of humble origin, that probably his family was very poor. So, it wasn't necessary to be born a nobleman or rich to succeed in life. There are other qualities which also lead to success. Courage, perseverance, the ability to dream and to persevere."*
>
> **Soichiro Honda**

2. Ratan Tata (1937–)

Ratan Tata is a former chairman of Tata Sons and chairman of Tata Group. According to Indiatimes.com's "11 Inspiring stories of people who bounced back after failing," Ratan was planning to sell the Tata Indica car project to Bill Ford but he did not go ahead with the sale because Bill Ford said to him "Why did you enter into the passenger car business when you had no knowing of it? It will be a favour if we buy this business from you." A few years later when Ford was in financial difficulty, Tata group purchased Jaguar-Land Rover from Ford. This time Bill Ford said to Ratan Tata, "You are doing a big favour for us by buying Jaguar-Land Rover".

> *"I do not know how history will judge me, but let me say that I've spent a lot of time and energy trying to transform the Tatas from a patriarchal concern to an institutional enterprise. It would, therefore, be a mark of failure on my part if it were perceived that Ratan Tata epitomises the Group's success. What I have done is establish growth mechanisms, play down individuals and play up the team that has made the companies what they are. I, for one, am not the kind who loves dwelling on the 'I'. If history remembers me at all, I hope it will be for this transformation.*
> *"*
>
> **Ratan Tata**

3. J. K. Rowling (1965–)

J K Rowling is a British author of the Harry Potter books and blockbuster films. According to Indiatimes.com's "11 Inspiring stories of people who bounced back after failing," there was a time in her life where she did not have a job, was divorced and didn't have any money to take care of her child. After her divorce she started writing the Harry Potter books. She had difficulty in getting the first book published, receiving about twelve rejections from publishing businesses. Two years later, she finally got her books published by Bloomsbury.

> *"The knowledge that you have emerged wiser and stronger from setbacks means that you are, ever after, secure in your ability to survive. You will never truly know yourself, or the strength of your relationships, until both have been tested by adversity.*
> *Such knowledge is a true gift, for all that it is painfully won, and it has been worth more than any qualification I ever earned."*
>
> ## J. K. Rowling

4. Anurag Kashyap (1972–)

Anurag Kashyap's is a controversial Indian film director. According to Indiatimes.com's "11 Inspiring stories of people who bounced back after failing," life was so tough when he first came to Bombay that he slept on the street because he had no money to rent a place to live. Most of his movies are films set in real life locations so the movies are low budget. He experienced a lot of unexpected issues from his first three movies.

- *Paanch* is a crime thriller that was not released. Anurag said in Unbumf.com "If Paanch had been released, I wouldn't have been half of what I am today,"

- *Black Friday* movie – according to Unbumf.com "Its release was delayed due to Bombay High Court's stay due to the impending bomb blast case judgment…"

- *No Smoking* has had mixed responses with mostly negative reviews.

- *Dev D* and *Gangs of Wasseypur* are successful and also have had an impact on the way Bollywood makes movies.

5. **Manoj Bhargava (1953–)**

Manoj Bhargava, an Indian American, was a monk first then became a billionaire businessman in the US. According to Youtube.com/watch?v=KG9rPTNFyTE and Youtube.com/watch?v=CyBHaF RSjl, he is the founder of Innovations Venture LLC which makes a 5-hour energy drink. His other products are involved in electricity and water filtration. Manoj has Ten Rules for Success as follows:

Minimize risk

Enjoy your work

Do something useful

Do your maximum today

Think with your head

Make slam dunk products

Avoid aggravation

Don't chase money

Think things through

Keep it simple

> *"My choice was to ruin my son's life by giving him money or giving 90-plus percent to charity."*
> *Not much of a choice.*
>
> **Manoj Bhargava**

6. Steve Jobs (1955–2011)

Steve Paul Jobs' unwed biological parents (Joanne Schieble and Abdulfattah Jandali) gave him up for adoption to a lower-middle class couple (Paul and Clara Jobs). He became a millionaire at 23. According to allaboutstevejobs.com's "Steve Jobs grew up in a neighbourhood of engineers working on electronics and other gizmos in their garages on weekends. This shaped his interest in the field as he grew up. At age 13, he met one the most important persons in his life: 18-year-old Stephen Wozniak, an electronics wiz kid, and, like Steve, an incorrigible prankster…" On 1 April 1976, they set up a company to make the Apple Computer in Steve Jobs' garage and sold to various computer dealers. Later Steve was kicked out by Apple, so he worked on his other projects including NeXt and Pixar before he came back to Apple.

"Getting fired from Apple was the best thing that could have ever happened to me. The heaviness of being successful was replaced by the lightness of being a beginner again, less sure about everything. It freed me to enter one of the most creative periods of my life."

Stanford 2005 Commencement Address, Steve Jobs, 12 Jun 2005

"Somebody once told me, 'Manage the top line, and the bottom line will follow.' What's the top line? It's things like, why are we doing this in the first place? What's our strategy? What are customers saying? How responsive are we? Do we have the best products and the best people? Those are the kind of questions you have to focus on."

The Entrepreneur of the Decade, Bo Burlingham, Inc. Magazine, 1 Apr 1989

7. Chris Gardner (1954–)

Chris Gardner is the author of the book of the *Pursuit of Happyness* movie according to Indiatimes.com's "11 Inspiring stories of people who bounced back after failing." He is an African-American self-made millionaire, investor, and stockbroker. He has lived in poverty and had been homeless during his life, which influenced his decision to provide assistance of $50 million to a project in San Francisco building housing for low income and unemployed people. He selected this area because it was a place of homelessness in his life that he lived before.

> *"If you have a dream and a desire to pursue it with every fibre of your being, but can't move past excuses or circumstances that seem to be standing in your way, there is a life lesson ahead with your name on it. If you are tired of the status quo and are dying to shake up your life, reinvent yourself, and find a pursuit you love doing so much that you can't wait for the sun to come up in the morning, you've come to the right place. If"*
> Chris Gardner,
> *Start Where You Are: Life Lessons in Getting from Where You Are to Where You Want to Be*

8. **Walt Disney (1901–1966)**

Walt Disney was a successful animator of the well- known Mickey Mouse cartoons and founder of amusement parks Disneyland and Disney World. According to biography. com, Walt Disney, in 1923 he declared bankruptcy and had numerous failures before he became successful.

> *"Mickey Mouse popped out of my mind onto a drawing pad 20 years ago on a train ride from Manhattan to Hollywood at a time when business fortunes of my brother Roy and myself were at our lowest ebb and disaster seemed right around the corner."*
>
> **Walt Disney**

9. **Henry Ford (1863–1947)**

Henry Ford was the founder of Ford Motor Company. According to bankruptcyhuntsville.com, Henry Ford's bankruptcy, he went bankrupt twice before he became successful.

> "You can do anything if you have enthusiasm. Enthusiasm is the yeast that makes your hopes rise to the stars. Enthusiasm is the spark in your eye, the swing in your gait, the grip of your hand, the irresistible surge of your will and your energy to execute your ideas. Enthusiasts are fighters, they have fortitude, and they have strong qualities. Enthusiasm is at the bottom of all progress. With it there is accomplishment. Without it there are only alibis."
>
> **Henry Ford**

10. Thomas Edison (1847–1931)

Thomas Edison is one of the greatest inventors of all time. He had a number of successes as well as failed inventions, but this did not stop him from continuing to carry on with his inventions. His light bulb contributed enormously to the electricity system of today. For more information see thomasedison.com.

> "I have not failed. I've just found 10,000 ways that won't work."
>
> **Thomas A. Edison**

11. Donald Trump (1946–)

Donald Trump is the 45th president of the United States from 2016 to today. Before he became US president, he was a successful businessman and television personality. His companies declared bankruptcy four times according to Atebits.com's "How to bounce back from bankruptcy: 10 famous people to guide you out of bad finances." ThoughtCo.com's "Donald-trump-bankruptcies" mentioned he filed bankruptcy in 1991 for Trump Taj Mahal and in 1992 for Trump Castle Hotel, Trump Plaza Casino, and Trump Plaza Hotel. Businessinsider.com's "Famous people who bounced back after being broke or bankrupt" states that Donald Trump has no bankruptcy record under his personal name. However, Trump's companies have declared bankruptcy six times in the years 1991, 1992, 2004 and 2009. The following words are taken from the Businessinsider.com article "I've cut debt – the way, this isn't me personally, it's a company." Trump said, according to Forbes, "Basically, I've used the laws of the country to my advantage… just as many, many others on top of the business world have."

"I'm competitive, and I love to create challenges for myself.
Maybe that's not always a good thing. It can make life complicated."
Donald Trump

---

12. Abraham Lincoln (1809–1865)

Abraham Lincoln was the 16th president of the United States in 1861. Businessinsider.com's "Famous people who bounced back after being broke or bankrupt" states that in 1823 Abraham brought a general store but the business was not doing well. When his business partner passed away, Lincoln had a debt of (£766) which was considered to be a large amount at the time. There was no bankruptcy law in those days, so he lost his horse and some equipment. He finally paid off his debt in 1840.

> *"You cannot escape the responsibility of tomorrow by evading it today."*
> **Abraham Lincoln**

13. Keith Urban (1967–)

Keith Urban is a singer, and was one of the Judges on *American Idol*. Sobernation.com's "5 Celebrities who have bounced back from a relapse" states that he has been to rehab a few times to help him overcome addictions to cocaine and alcohol. He has been successful in overcoming the addictions.

> *"There was never a time I became interested in what I do -- I truly believe it was pre-determined before I even came along. Music runs through my family history, and it's as natural to me as breathing."*
> **Keith Urban**

How to bounce back from setbacks?

Bouncing back from setbacks is not easy and it isn't something that's straightforward. The reality is that not everyone is able to have the inner strength, desire and the resources to start over again. It can be concluded from the above 14 real life stories that successful and famous people worldwide do not allow defeat to deaden their spirit and they won't allow setbacks to stop them from achieving their goals.

> *"It doesn't matter how many times you have setbacks. It doesn't matter how painful and costly those failures and setbacks are.*
> *What matters is not to give up on yourself, and pick yourself right back up again to create the foundation of greatness and so you may make a name for yourself."*

1. Have the right support such as a mentor to help you in your journey.

2. Have focus, determination, and persistence in achieving your passions and goals.

3. Learn and improve from setbacks. Over time you achieve goals and it may be an even better and bigger dream than you imagined when you first worked on your goals. It might take longer and not within the timeframe that you would like to see. It may be a blessing in disguise, because new avenues will open up offering unexpected gains in a new direction. You may make a name for yourself too.

4. Accept the situation and be honest with yourself that things are not working out as planned, don't pretend, or talk yourself into believing that you didn't want that goal in the first place.

5. Think with your head more than your heart and this will help you to see things clearer. It is best that your logical thinking is in line with the emotional reasons for doing things.

6. Not being able to achieve your goals is tough and there is hurt associated with setbacks, but do not allow yourself to focus on the setbacks and failure forever.

7. Have procedures and systems to prevent making the same mistake again

8. Know your reasons "Why" you want to achieve the goals and make sure it's a good reason. If the reasons you want to achieve something are strong enough, you will find a way to achieve your goals in the end.

AUTHOR'S FINAL WORD

I hope that the information and case studies have resonated deep in your mind, heart and soul and they motivate you to take action and not give up on your dreams and goals.

> *"Never mind what the "people' think of you! They may overestimate or underestimate you! Until they discover your real worth, your success depends mainly upon what you think of yourself and whether you believe in yourself. You can succeed if nobody believes it; but you will never succeed if you don't believe in yourself"*
> **William J. H. Boetcker**

Wishing you success in life
Good luck

Thu Le Huynh

"Helping you to have more cash, customers and clients."

ABOUT THE AUTHOR

BUSINESS ADVISOR, PROFIT STRATEGIST AND ACCOUNTANT

Thu Le Huynh is a business advisor and the founder of Total Care Accounting Solutions & Total Care Accounting and Business Solutions. Her business clients come from a diverse range of industries.

Born in Vietnam, Thu became an orphan at 11 before moving to Australia where she learned English in high school. After studying science at Australian university and starting her career in the pharmaceutical industry, she made a career transition by studying at nights and on the weekends to complete her Master of Taxation, Certificate in Professional Accounting, Certificate IV Finance Services (Bookkeeping), and Certificate IV Small Business Management. She also completed a Business Advisor Training Programme, Mastermind.com Professional, and earned the official title of Knowledge Broker.

She worked for several tax agents' practices before branching out to start her own award-winning tax and accounting business. Thu is now in demand. She assists business owners to increase their revenue, get more customers and clients, increase profits, minimise their tax and put processes and systems into place.

Thu is a member of the National Tax and Accountants' Association (NTAA). She has a keen interest in share trading.

She has travelled to various Australian cities and country areas, including walking part of the Bibbulmun Track in WA, and has travelled to Singapore and Malaysia.

She has also had dogs all her life.

Thu is the author of *The Business Advisor* and she currently lives in Perth, Australia.

RECOMMENDED RESOURCES:

RECOMMENDED RESOURCES:

Being a small business owner relies on a mixture of your street smarts, intelligence, knowledge, experience and adventure and I love being able to share that with other business owners.

To find out more about our taxation, advisory, business growth, accounting and other services, visit our website:

www.TotalCareAccountingSolutions.com.au

REFERENCES

The Forbes Book of Business Quotations edited by Ted Goodman

The 10 Day Turnaround How To Transform Your Business Virtually

Overnight… by Spike Humer and Darren J Stephens

Business Dynamics by Tim Atterton

https://www.abc.net.au/news/2015-08-24/wangara-factory-fire-damage-bill-estimated-at-12-million/6720106

https://www.theguardian.com/money/2012/apr/24/how-avoid-paying-tax-maximise-income

https://www.theguardian.com/money/shortcuts/2012/may/01/stephen-king-pay-more-tax

https://www.acnc.gov.au/for-public/charity-tax-concessions/my-donation-tax-deductible

https://www.ato.gov.au/Business/GST/Tax-invoices/

https://www.smh.com.au/business/bunnings-caught-up-in-massive-tradie-tax-fraud-amid-calls-for-abn-overhaul-20170802-gxnmz4.html

https://www.smh.com.au/national/australian-tax-system-complex-survey-20080619-2tgj.html

https://www.ato.gov.au/General/The-fight-against-tax-crime/News-and-results/Case-studies/Tax-crime-prosecution-case-studies/

https://www.findlaw.com.au/articles/4226/what-is-a-testamentary-trust-and-should-i-have-one.aspx

https://www.ato.gov.au/Business/Privately-owned-and-wealthy-groups/Tax-governance/Estate-planning/

https://www.entrepreneur.com/article/78778

https://estate.findlaw.com/wills/top-ten-reasons-to-have-a-will.html

https://www.choice.com.au/health-and-body/healthy-ageing/ageing-and-retirement/articles/enduring-power-of-attorney

https://asic.gov.au/about-asic/corporate-publications/newsletters/infocus/infocus-october-2019-volume-28-issue-9/#Scams

https://www.azquotes.com/author/7682-Franz_Kafka

https://www.biography.com/writer/franz-kafka

https://www.biography.com/us-president/bill-clinton

https://www.azquotes.com/quote/543463

https://procrastinus.com/procrastination/famous-procrastinators/

https://www.psychologytoday.com/us/articles/200308/procrastination-ten-things-know

https://www.brainyquote.com/quotes/victor_hugo_152564

https://www.leonardodavinci.net/quotes.jsp

https://quotes.thefamouspeople.com/bill-clinton-848.php

https://www.goodreads.com/author/quotes/1624.Herman_Melville

https://www.notablebiographies.com/Jo-Ki/Johnson-Samuel.html

https://www.goodreads.com/work/quotes/1885548-the-tragicall-historie-of-hamlet-prince-of-denmark

https://succeedfeed.com/jeff-bezos-quotes/

https://www.goalcast.com/2017/12/07/27-bill-gates-quotes/

https://hbr.org/2000/03/how-to-fight-a-price-war

https://hedgescompany.com/blog/2010/10/formula-price-increase-price-decrease/

References

https://www.business.vic.gov.au/money-profit-and-accounting/pricing/Discount-strategies

https://www.business.vic.gov.au/case-studies/how-to-discount-for-business-growth

https://www.allianzlife.com/about/news-and-events/news-releases/Longevity-study-launch-press-release

https://www.msn.com/en-au/lifestyle/smart-living/50-most-common-regrets-people-have-in-their-50s/ss-AADotNW?li=AAgfLCP

https://www.entrepreneur.com/article/280134

https://www.careeraddict.com/top-10-most-famous-procrastinators-in-the-world

https://www.inc.com/john-rampton/10-reasons-why-a-mentor-is-a-must.html

https://medium.com/swlh/whats-the-difference-between-a-mentor-an-advisor-and-a-coach-b72165bba983

http://www.trajectify.com/blog/2015/1/25/the-difference-between-coaches-mentors

https://www.referralcandy.com/blog/company-culture-examples/

https://www.thrill.com.au/team-building-case-study/

https://thefruitfultoolbox.com/case-study-microsoft-team-building-and-group-dynamics/

https://acronyms.thefreedictionary.com/TEAM

https://www.indiatimes.com/culture/who-we-are/11-inspiring-stories-of-people-who-bounced-back-after-failing-269768.html

https://www.britannica.com/biography/Honda-Soichiro

https://addicted2success.com/quotes/40-motivational-soichiro-honda-quotes/

https://unbumf.com/anurag-kashyap-a-fearless-filmmaker-who-made-a-mark-on-his-own-terms/

https://www.youtube.com/watch?v=KG9rPTNFyTE

https://www.youtube.com/watch?v=CyBHaF_RSjI

https://openquotes.github.io/authors/manoj-bhargava-quotes/

https://allaboutstevejobs.com/

Stanford 2005 Commencement Address, Steve Jobs, 12 Jun 2005

https://answersafrica.com/chris-gardner-homeless-multi-millionaire.html

https://www.goodreads.com/author/quotes/7127.Chris_Gardner

https://www.biography.com/business-figure/walt-disney

https://www.brainyquote.com/quotes/walt_disney_131658

https://bankruptcyhuntsville.com/blog/henry-fords-bankruptcy/

http://www.thomasedison.com/

https://www.thoughtco.com/donald-trump-business-bankruptcies-4152019

https://www.atebits.com/how-to-bounce-back-from-bankruptcy-10-famous-people-to-guide-you-out-of-bad-finances/

https://www.businessinsider.com/famous-people-who-bounced-back-after-being-broke-or-bankrupt-2017-7/?r=AU&IR=T

http://www.top10-best.com/k/top_10_best_keith_urban_quotes.html